All Over the Map

Also by

Laura Fraser

An Italian Affair

Losing It

All Over

Laura Fraser

the Map

Harmony Books / New York

Portions of this book originally appeared in *Elle; More; O, The Oprah Magazine;*
the *New York Times; Marie Claire; Gourmet; Eating Well;* and Salon.com.

Library of Congress Cataloging-in-Publication Data
Fraser, Laura.
All over the map / Laura Fraser.—1st ed.
1. Fraser, Laura. 2. Fraser, Laura—Travel. 3. Single women—United
States—Biography. 4. Man-woman relationships—United States.
5. Women authors, American—Biography. 6. Travel writers—United
States—Biography. 7. San Francisco (Calif.)—Biography. 8. Americans—
Mexico—San Miguel de Allende—Biography. 9. San Miguel de Allende
(Mexico)—Biography. I. Title.
CT275.F6949A3 2010
810.9'9287—dc22
[B]
2009045251
ISBN 978-0-307-45063-0

Printed in the United States of America

Design by Lynne Amft

Maps by Mapping Specialists Ltd.

10 9 8 7 6 5 4 3 2 1

First Edition

To my mother, Virginia H. Fraser

Of course I should love to throw a toothbrush into a bag, and just go, quite vaguely, without any plans or even a real destination. It is the Wanderlust.

—VITA SACKVILLE-WEST, *Letters*

You never know when you're making a memory.

—RICKIE LEE JONES, "Young Blood"

All Over the Map

The winter sun warms the cobblestones that pave the Plaza de Armas in Oaxaca, Mexico. Heavy colonial archways shade the café tables where travelers and people watchers and expatriates come to just sit. They sip their coffees and take in the scene: small boys hawking huge bunches of colorful balloons, musicians in worn suits and perfectly ironed shirts stopping off for a shoe shine, ancient-faced Indians carrying baskets of greens on their heads. Beyond the *zócalo,* the Sierra Madre mountain range rings the town. There is no hurry here.

The atmosphere is relaxed, but inside I'm buzzing like one of the bees at the fruit vendor's cart. I glance around the plaza, eyes barely resting on the balconies, the bandstand, the laurel trees, the women with dark braids and bright embroidered tops perched on the edge of the fountain. I check my watch, and it isn't even time yet.

I've come to Oaxaca to mark my fortieth birthday, the passing of the decade during which I probably should have gotten married (again) and had children but did not. It didn't work out that way. But I am going to celebrate anyway, celebrate the fact that I have the freedom to run off and be in Mexico for my birthday; celebrate with someone—a friend? lover?—for whom all of life is a celebration if you just find the right spot in the sun to sit and take it all in.

I close my eyes to calm myself and sense the faint whiffs of chocolate, coffee, and chiles that perfume the thin air. When I open my eyes, I catch sight of him across the plaza: his soft denim jacket, thick silver bracelet, and chestnut curls that somehow, still, are not gray. I jump up and wave wildly, and he sees me— everyone sees me—and he drops his old leather suitcase and opens his arms wide.

In a moment, I am pressing my face against his, breathing in his familiar smell of cigars and sea, amazed, as always, to see him again. I met this man, the Professor, by chance over breakfast in a *pensione* on an Italian island four years ago, right after my husband left me. Over the course of those years, meeting every so often in a different city or island, he helped mend my heart. He has his life and I have mine, but every time we're together, the scenery seems brighter and the flavors more intense.

"*Professore,*" I say, breaking our embrace to search his face.

"*Laura,*" he says, with the soft rolling Italian pronunciation, which could also be Spanish. I like my name, and maybe myself, better in a Latin country. It's softer.

The Professor sits at the café, orders coffee, and moves his chair close, positioning his face in the sun. He squeezes my hand. "*Bel posto,*" he says. Beautiful place.

"*Incantado,*" I say, not sure, as often happens, if I am speaking Italian or Spanish. Enchanted.

"*La bella vita continua,*" he says.

He tells me that I look as good as ever, and I say he looks even better, something has changed. He seems energetic and expansive for his normally cool Parisian aesthetics professor self, less pale. He is brimming with a secret joy.

By the time we walk several blocks back to our hotel, opening the door onto a promiscuous jungle of a garden, he has spilled the whole story. He finally split up with the wife who didn't love him, who had been in love with someone else for years. And he's found an exciting new relationship.

We sit at a colorful little tile table on the patio outside our room, and he tells me everything. I've known there have been other women between our rendezvous, and there have been other men for me, too. But I'm not sure I want to hear all this. I don't care to know, for instance, that she is Eastern European and a professor herself and teaches comparative literature. Even less that she probably spends more on her lingerie than her clothes. While he tells his story I stare at a banana tree, counting the leaves from the bottom, struggling to be able to say, by the time I reach the clear sky above, that I am happy for him instead of sorry for myself. It's not as if I'd ever imagined that I would end up in Paris with the Professor. Well, not very often. I did start taking French.

"I'm happy for you," I say finally, and I'm glad, at least, to see that adds to his joy. I'm trying not to think about how ironic it is that it is the Professor—the rogue, the adventurer, the Don Juan—who is happy to be settling down, while I, the one who has wanted a steady partner, a companion, a house and family, am sharing a hotel room with yet another man who likes me a lot and is not in love with me. If he says we can always be friends, I will lose it completely.

I turn the key to our whitewashed room, and he flops down on the carved wooden bed. I lie next to him, fighting tears, and he caresses my cheek. Then he strokes the small of my back.

I roll away and sit up. "Professor," I finally say, "it's too hard for me to be friends who tell each other everything about their love lives and still be lovers."

"Not for me," he says, sexy as ever.

I push his hand away and sigh. "Let's go eat."

I CHOSE OAXACA for my birthday and convinced the Professor to join me (before this new romance of his) because I happened across a book by Italo Calvino, *Under the Jaguar Sun,* in which each essay is devoted to one of the senses. Of all the cities in the world where Calvino had dined—and he was Italian, mind you—for him Oaxaca embodied the ultimate fulfillment of the sense of taste. Oaxacan cuisine, he wrote, mixes a cornucopia of native vegetables with spices and recipes brought over by the Spanish. Over the centuries, those cuisines were mingled, enhanced, and perfected by cloistered nuns (for whom cooking was one of the few earthly indulgences). Calvino called Oaxacan food "an elaborate and bold cuisine" with flavor notes that vibrate against one another in harmonies and dissonances to "a point of no return, an absolute possession exercised on the receptivity of all the senses."

Ah, yes. For now, in Oaxaca, with the Professor, the food will have to do all the stirring of the senses.

And so we eat. We venture to a modest place near the hotel

where a stout woman does wonders in the tiny kitchen. We try dishes that are familiar by name but taste unlike any Mexican food I've ever eaten. The guacamole is fresher, the tortillas sweeter and crisper. The dark sauce on the enchiladas and chiles rellenos seem concocted from an ancient, mysterious alchemy. For the French Professor, who has never set foot in this country before and has tried Mexican food only secondhand in San Francisco when he visited me there, every taste is new.

For the next few days, we explore Oaxaca's cuisine, trying moles in different colors each day—from Amarillo, with tomatillos and chiles, to a black, chocolaty mole negro. Each sauce requires days to prepare, and each bite is a layered, earthy, mouth-warming experience. The Professor sighs, watching me in anticipation of the pleasure of my bite, and then I sigh with him, adding the layers and spices of our history and passion to each complicated mouthful.

Between meals, we visit Monte Alban, the Zapotec ruins, climbing to the top of the pyramids to take in the wide sky and view of the town below. You can see why Hernán Cortés, who was offered anywhere in Mexico for himself after his conquest, chose the Oaxaca Valley. Then we walk all the way back to town to find Aztec soup and chicken tamales wrapped in banana leaves. We wander around the neat cobblestone streets another day, peeking into brightly painted churches, admiring cactus gardens, browsing in art galleries—and then we order Anaheim and poblano chiles sautéed with fresh cheese, onions, and crème fraiche. We tour Oaxaca's huge food market, pass stalls with hanging pigs, fresh chocolate, stacks of cactus, and basketfuls of corn, tomatoes, onions, exotic greens, and roasted grasshoppers. Tidy piles of chiles stand as tall as I. We discover the chocolate factory and drink creamy hot chocolate, looking into each other's eyes, bittersweet.

"*Qué rico,*" I say to the server as I finish my chocolate. How delicious.

"How do you know Spanish?" the Professor asks.

I explain that my mother brought my three older sisters and me to live in Mexico for a summer when I was ten years old. We spent that time in San Miguel de Allende, a colonial town not unlike Oaxaca, at an age when I was unafraid to roam around and try to talk to everyone. It was when I got my first taste of the wide world and felt a hunger for its endless sights and flavors. It was also when I first understood that being able to speak another language, even the few phrases one can manage at ten, isn't just a matter of translating familiar words; it's a way of expanding your internal territory and venturing outside the borders of your culture and family. The fresh new sentences change the very nature of your thoughts, your usual reactions, and your sense of who you are. I learned, that summer, that I couldn't speak a little Spanish without becoming a little Mexican. That exciting summer in San Miguel de Allende—discovering the pleasures of discovery—was when I first became a traveler.

"Intelligent mother," says the Professor, pushing back from the table, content.

EVENTUALLY IT IS our last evening, and we have finished dinner down to the mescal, satiated with the place, cheeks warmed, and cheerful, for the moment, with our transition to friends.

"Happy birthday," says the Professor, and he pulls out a necklace he bought from an Indian vendor, a lovely string of turquoise and amber. I try to remember if any man besides my father has ever bought me a piece of jewelry. Aside from my first boyfriend in college, who gave me an opal pendant as a parting gift, I can't recall any. I was outraged once when my friend Giovanna told me her husband had never bought her any jewelry during their entire marriage, with all the toys he bought for himself, and maybe I was so mad because mine didn't, either. So this gift, at forty, is a delightful surprise. The Professor clasps it, hands warm, on my neck. "What do you wish for?"

So many things. I wish we could stay in Oaxaca and be the lovers we used to be. I wish I could still fall in love or even believe I could. I wish for great food, adventure, and soul-scorching sex. Maybe a child, still. I wish for it all.

"Romance and adventure," I say. I do not say what else I wish for, maybe what I wish for most, because it seems contrary to everything else, which is to be with one man or in one place, to have something settled in a life where nothing is settled.

"Do you think you can have both?" asks the Professor. "Who is the man who will let you roam around the world, meeting your old lovers?"

I shrug. "Maybe he'll travel with me."

"Good luck," says the Professor, and he is sincere.

I twirl my glass between my fingers, sniff the smoky mescal, and wonder, as I always wonder, whether we will see each other again. I ask the Professor if he thinks we might travel together again.

"You never know," he says. He reaches over and strokes my

hand. *"La vita è bella e lunga,"* he says. Life is beautiful and long. We clink glasses.

After dinner, we go back to the hotel and snuggle together like contented old friends.

"Buenas noches," I tell him, and he is already snoozing.

I can't sleep. The moon is peeking through the wooden window frame, and I wonder about my wishes for romance and adventure. This man I have loved, off and on, is leaving tomorrow, and, as usual, I don't know when or whether I'll see him again. The men in my life are always like the countries I visit: I fall in love briefly and then move on. I visit, regard the wonders, delve into the history, taste the cooking, peer into dark corners, feel a few moments of excitement and maybe ecstasy and bliss, and then, though I am often sad to leave—or stung that no one insists that I stay—I am on my way.

Here on a sultry night in a foreign country, with a man sleeping next to me, casually throwing his skinny leg over my soft one, I realize I don't have someone whom I can call home. I wonder if it's possible to have everything I wished for on my fortieth birthday: adventure and romance, wanderlust and just plain lust.

I turn in the bed. Actually, it isn't exactly romance and lust that I wish for. Finding a fascinating and attractive man on the road, going from being perfect strangers to holding hands, sharing stories and bites of dessert, gazing into each other's eyes over dinner, and then stopping for a moment to stare at each other again in bed—that's romance, that's lust. That's exciting and wonderful, but it's all too brief, like a vacation. Of course, you can travel the world and find romance. What's more elusive is real companionship, someone who's always making the same dent on his side of the bed, who knows how you like your coffee in the morning. It's much harder to find comfort and stability, to be held, to be secure in the knowledge that someone is taking care of you and even—old-fashioned as it sounds—protecting you.

You can't grow old with someone if you're always off searching for new experiences. And I'm not getting any younger.

I roll over again, facing the Professor, who echoes my disturbance with a few deep, skidding snores. I'm restless and agitated. I face the Professor and then turn toward the wall; I don't feel comfortable anywhere. My desires—to be free and to belong, to be independent and to be inextricably loved, to be in motion and to be still—pull me back and forth. The Professor sleeps soundly while I wrestle with the two sides of myself until I am worn out and the moonlight dims, replaced by the cool light of dawn.

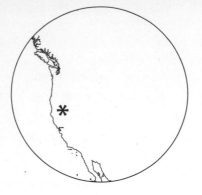

Chapter Two

SAN FRANCISCO *
CANYONLANDS
NATIONAL PARK

2OOI

H ome from Oaxaca, I drop my bags in my San Francisco flat and suddenly everything seems urgent—sorting the mail, straightening the house, finding a man, having a kid.

For four years I've tabled the issue of settling down by having an affair with a romantic Frenchman who was available only for jaunts to Italian islands, British art museums, or Moroccan medinas, not for buying groceries or paying the gas bill. At the time, that suited me fine: he brought me back to myself after a painful divorce, made me feel desired again, and helped me experience the simple pleasures of the sunset, the sea, grilled calamari, reading on a hammock with someone, a midnight swim. He took care of me when we were together, and even apart, he let me know that someone on the other side of the world was always thinking of me. But now he, of all people, has settled down, leaving me—at forty—with only my independence for company, along with more wrinkles and severely decreased chances of fertility.

I suppose I knew all along that having a part-time international lover was a temporary solution. You can't go on buying plane tickets forever, treating your life at home as if it's dead time between vacations, always living in anticipation of being with somebody somewhere else. At a certain point you want to wake up with your head on your own pillow and have that somebody be snoozing right next to you.

That's what I always assumed would happen, anyway, and it catches me by surprise to be alone at this age. In my twenties and thirties I figured I would find someone as full of wanderlust as I am, and we'd intersperse our forays into foreign cultures with intimate nights at home, making risotto and pulling out a special bottle of Italian wine on a regular Tuesday. Turning the corner of my twenties, I met a fellow journalist whose Italian grandparents made their own wine and who let me know from the start that tofu is no substitute for gnocchi. Our four-year relationship seemed to promise that, it would always be possible to mix adventure and comfy domesticity. We were similar physical types—sturdy, energetic dirty blonds who love to eat just a smidge more than we love to exercise—and both game to take off for a train trip through Italy, to mountain bike in the red rock canyons of Utah, or hike in the high Colorado wilderness. We were just as happy to stay home, spending an evening rolling out homemade linguine, inviting friends over, or lounging around drinking beer and watching basketball. I might have been more interested in the hiking than the hoops, but it evened out.

That relationship ended during that odd phase women have in their early thirties when they think they have no time left but all the time in the world: I wanted to get married and have a child right away, yet, when Leo was more than ambivalent—my frustration pushed him further away—I also thought I still had plenty of years to run into someone even more exciting to settle down with. I believed that the balance of exotic travel and cozy home life I found living with Leo would always be easy to find. And though there's little I regret about our relationship or breakup— we had a wonderful four years, parted amicably for good reasons, and always wish each other well—I only now appreciate that whatever else we had together, that balance was rare.

No sooner had Leo and I contemplated splitting up than I was off with another man, who dazzled me with his wit, intelligence, and brilliant smile. He was smitten, lavishing attention on me like a spotlight illuminating my best self. The fact that I loved to travel seemed to make me all that much more fascinating to him; my Italian friend Lucia couldn't understand how we could love each other and be apart for an entire month while I studied in Florence, yet he seemed more ardent than ever when I returned, speaking better Italian. But when we set off into marriage, a journey for life, I didn't realize he had a return ticket hidden in his back pocket. It turned out that all the qualities that had initially attracted him—my exuberance, my independence— were exactly the things, in the end, he admitted, that he'd wanted to extinguish. Then he turned that spotlight of his, that projection, onto someone else, someone he'd grown up with, who felt more like home to him.

Now I've been divorced for about four years, and it takes a good couple of years to get over losing the guy you thought you'd be holding hands with through old age and to rouse yourself from a crushing depression when you never thought you were the kind of person who could be depressed in the first place. Being with the Professor during that difficult time was like having a luxury liner float me over choppy seas, all the while sitting up on deck in lounge chairs drinking wine and watching the stars, impervious to the waves, then landing safely on the other shore.

But now on the other side is forty, the most foreign place I've ever visited, and suddenly I'm all by myself. They take your passport at the gate, confront you with a clipboard, and ask, "Where is your husband?" and "When, by the way, are you going to have kids?"

Consult the map. Get your bearings. I manage to change money, catch the bus, find a meal and a pensione by nightfall in most foreign countries. How hard can it be, finding a husband, a house, a family at forty? You just have to set out in the right direction. Who knows: for all the bleak wilderness here I might stumble across something unexpected and delightful, something I didn't even know I was looking for.

So I take off walking. Right away, I realize I'm completely unprepared for this place; everyone else seems to have a house, spouse, children, and a retirement plan, and I've only thought to pack sunscreen, a water bottle, and a good book. I take in the sights, the new terrain, and over there I see the loss of youthful good looks that I can no longer afford to dress down. I wander in another direction, and I see my precociousness losing its early blossoms, flowers fading; I haven't accomplished what my young, spectacular, A+ successes predicted. I look around at the houses, and I notice that I'm still renting; I haven't managed to own one by now. Over there, I watch toddlers chasing butterflies at the

playground, and—it's something in the air here—my eyes well
up with tears.

Which direction to go in? House, husband, child? I have
no idea. Since I got divorced, friends have asked why I don't go
ahead and have a kid on my own, adopt a baby from one of those
Third World countries I'm always visiting. But I'm not one of
those people who always knew I had to have children. I always
knew I wanted to be like Brenda Starr, ace reporter, traveling
the world, having liaisons with the mysterious, one-eyed Basil St.
John, playing gotcha with evil heads of corporations. If I found the
right man, it would be a wonderful adventure to have kids; but
if that guy didn't show up, it wouldn't be a tragedy, it would just
be a different kind of adventure. Even if, deep down, I always assumed that I'd wake up one day with a baby bouncing on the bed,
I can't do it on my own—especially given my personality, which
is not the most patient and stable one in the world—because it
wouldn't be fair to the child, who would deserve two parents. It
wouldn't be fair to me, either; I would wither without some help
and a little taste of freedom now and then.

I'M STARING AT my suitcase, not yet unzipped, full of dirty
sundresses and jungle pants, trying to figure out where to go next.
I finger my turquoise-and-amber necklace, parting gift. The
truth is that I don't have the first clue where to look for a new
man or a new life; I have so sense of direction whatsoever. I feel
too fragile to try to meet anyone new. I don't *want* to meet anyone
new. I want to rewind, go back to Oaxaca, back to that Mexican

garden, where the Professor would tell me in Italian that I'm the love of his life, I should come back to Paris, learn to speak French, and we could spend summers in a little house in southern Italy. I want my vacation to go on forever, to *be* my life. I wonder if the Professor ever suspected that's what I wanted; I wonder if I ever let him know.

The last thing I can do is sit here with these feelings. I have to get up and go somewhere, or I'll explode. I know I have a habit of running away from a broken heart and that it usually tags along. Maybe it's an addiction. But buying a plane ticket is a lot healthier than binge eating or drinking for heartache, and sometimes you can even manage to outrun it on the road.

I think about the first time I flew away from a disappointment in love, just after college. I was enchanted with a guy named Edward, who told me—kissing in the rain in Little Italy—that he was sorry, he just didn't love me. Crushed, I had to get away. I took an inheritance from my grandmother—$1,500—and left New York to travel around the Mediterranean by myself. My more practical older sisters used the money for a car or toward a down payment on a house, but I figured Grandma would've been tickled to know that I took the meager savings she'd been able to tuck away as a teacher and single mom and went off to Europe, the place where she'd had the jolliest time of her retirement, accompanied by her two best friends, dressing up in hats and gloves and big rhinestone earrings and taking tea in grand hotels as if they did it every day.

I flew to Greece and stayed as long as Grandma's money lasted, which was nine months, ten countries, Liron in Israel,

Antonio in Spain, and Julian in London. Each place presented new discoveries and passions, bright and fresh, that dulled the memory of that brief summer romance. I ate just-caught calamari grilled with ouzo, swam in hot springs after work on a kibbutz, went on a camel safari with Bedouins, climbed Mount Saint Catherine at sunset, danced flamenco in Seville, had a Turkish massage in Budapest, fell in love with Italy, and drove through sweet country villages in England. There, Julian was difficult to leave, tears streaming at the airport, but after living with him for a month in Hampstead Heath and getting a job waitressing in a pub, I realized I didn't want to live in London forever, that the journey couldn't stop there, not with him. (Recently I heard from Julian, who e-mailed to say he'd read a story I'd written about having an international affair: "We don't really change much, do we?")

That trip established my penchant for travel—with its endless art, food, languages, and people to explore—as a distraction from emotional pain. I also realized, publishing my first freelance feature article in the *Jerusalem Post* while I was living on a kibbutz, that you can justify the whole footloose business by writing a few stories along the way. And even when I don't muster up any serious work, when my career is hardly careening along as fast as it should be, here in my prime, going on trips can be a handy diversion from that very fact. It strikes me that when I'm traveling, I have stories to tell and postcards to send, and I appear to be accomplishing something in life just by going to exotic places. My friends with their husbands and children and carpools and Tater Tot tantrums think I'm lucky, I'm free, my life is immeasurably more interesting than theirs. Maybe I'm not churning out books, but I'm writing articles published in glossy magazines that they're happy to read when they finally get a chance to sit down to have their highlights done. It never crosses their minds that I might wish to have some of their cozy and boring stability.

At home, with my suitcase still unpacked, I'm afraid I've reached a point in my life where, despite all of my traveling, I am not moving at all.

I TALLY UP my frequent-flier miles and consider which friends I could stay with in foreign countries, then search around for tickets, but I can't come up with anything right. I'm perplexed. If I'm trying to escape my feelings about the person I used to rely on to escape my feelings—or if I'm running off from the uncomfortable realization that I'm always trying to run off—it all sort of cancels itself out. The only thing that's clear is that I need to go somewhere. But if I went to a foreign city with great museums and restaurants, I'd just miss the Professor.

The one place I could really lose him would be in the wilderness; he'd never find himself anywhere that doesn't sell Gitanes and a good espresso.

That's not such a bad idea. My parents used to send us kids off on character-building backpacking trips when we were in our teens, which—when we finally made it to the crest of a 14,000-foot Colorado peak, exhausted and exhilarated—really did improve our self-esteem. It's not just the physical challenge that's rejuvenating: in the mountains, you're stripped down to the essentials of who you are, a friendly human being out there among

the blue jays and deer, and you have no choice but to feel benevolent toward yourself and everyone else. Long before I had the
habit of traveling to foreign countries to restore myself, I used to
head to the wilderness.

. I recall how healing it was once, when I was a sophomore at
a sophisticated Eastern college—far from home and intimidated
by fellow students who seemed so worldly to me—to send out
a rescue mission for my lost happy self by spending a few days
hiking around in the Rockies. Right away, I could breathe better.
The thing about being out in the wild is that your angst seems so
small when you're surrounded by trees, rocks, and vast, sweeping
views. Hiking around, I realized that deep down, just between
me and the pine trees, I was absolutely fine. I might not be from
New York City, but Colorado smells a lot fresher. There was
a whole lot I didn't know, socially and culturally, about sharp,
monied people on the East Coast, but there's a lot that everyone
doesn't know outside their realm, no matter how smart they may
be—a realization that helped me later on as a journalist—and it's
better to admit to being naive and ask a lot of questions than to
pretend to be someone you aren't and end up acting like a jerk.
In the woods, you can't get away with being a jerk, especially to
yourself, which is what I had been doing. So I went back to school
and focused on what I wanted from college, not on what other
people were thinking about me or whether I was sophisticated
enough for them. When I returned to school after those days outdoors, I brought along my cowboy boots, and from then on, college was a great ride.

So that's it, then: back to nature. I'll leave it to the wide-open

West to mend my heart. I need to find some sort of organized wilderness program, such as a yoga hiking retreat, with massages, hot tubs, and gourmet vegetarian food.

I wander around my apartment and pick up my favorite photo of my mother, sitting on a slick red rock in Canyonlands, sunning her legs, dabs of sunscreen on her cheeks. I recall that when she was in her forties, craving adventure and some kind of personal growth, she signed up for Outward Bound, a notoriously difficult mountaineering program designed to build character via challenging wilderness encounters. She went to Utah's Capitol Reef National Park, a vast expanse of bloodred canyons and over-lapping rock ledges, to backpack and rock climb with a group of women. Since hers was the first-ever Outward Bound course designed just for women, a magazine writer went along. The fact that someone got paid to tag along on Mom's trip to write about it was not lost on me, even as a kid.

Curious, I discover that Outward Bound still exists and has a special one-week "Life and Career Renewal" course aimed at adults who feel stuck in their careers or relationships. Without thinking it through much further, I find a magazine to pay my way—to write a mother/daughter essay about challenging your-self at forty—and load up my backpack.

I FLY TO Grand Junction and am relieved to be back in familiar, wide-open territory, next to the Western Slope's red mesas with massive violet mountain ranges in the distance. The sky is Colorado blue, the air fresh, my hiking boots oiled, my sleeping bag stuffed, and I feel giddy. I can't wait to hike through narrow, smooth, terra-cotta canyons, scramble on rocks, crawl through arches, and forget about the fact that my heart feels as crumbly as sandstone.

Early the next morning, all the Outward Bound participants, most middle-aged and wearing fleece, gather outside the motel and climb aboard a school bus. I've nearly forgotten that this is a group experience, and seeing the others makes me nervous. I'm shy and awkward in small groups, especially when you are supposed to share your feelings. I almost always have the urge to bolt, say something too direct, or cry for no reason that anyone, including me, can fathom. My particular idea of hell is to spend eternity going around a circle in a small group to say who you are, where you're from, and what you want out of this experience—and right now, I can feel that coming on.

After a couple of hours on the bus, we arrive at a staging area, a mesa above the Needles section of Utah's magnificent Canyonlands National Park. On the ride, I've discovered that most of the others in my group—an institutional food company executive, a manager at a sock-manufacturing company, a venture capitalist, a Realtor, a computer programmer, and a timid, pale recent college graduate—have suffered the loss of a loved one, job, or relationship and are, like me, trying to work their way out of a serious funk. This Outward Bound trip seems like a desperately optimistic measure for just about everyone. A few in the group are in rather poor physical shape, and one gal seems to be verging on anorexia. There is no man in the group who I am going to fall in love with and tell the story of how we met on Outward Bound.

Our leader, Dennis, a thirty-two-year-old mountaineer who isn't in great emotional shape himself—he lost some friends climbing Denali a couple years back, gained a hundred pounds, and hasn't been back to the wilderness until now—has us, yes, go around in a circle and explain what we want from the experience. Fifty-year-old Tina, the socks manager, is struggling with the death of a close friend and trying to kick a thirty-year smoking habit, and says she came "in order to cry." The fifty-two-year-old Midwestern CEO, Bob, tells us he needs to have more fun in his life. The three women in their thirties are variously battling heartbreak, stress, and depression, and the thirty-one-year-old guy has just seen his dot-com dreams fizzle, along with his love life.

Now it's my turn. There's no way I'm going to go into the story of being divorced, having a love affair end, already missing the Professor, feeling stuck at forty, uncertain where to turn, and caught between wanting to travel and settle down. I muster up something vague but acceptably group-sharing about having a midlife crisis and needing to rearrange my goals. I smile nervously at the end, and Tina the socks manager says, "When you smile, everything about you changes—you seemed so tough and reserved before, and now you're warm and pretty," which is exactly the kind of comment I fear from a stranger in a small group.

Just as my eyes tear, Dennis switches gears, announcing our first wilderness lesson. He demonstrates how to take care of our private business in the great outdoors. I didn't expect this to be quite so Outdoors 101; I thought we'd be rappelling one another

off of cliffs by now. Dennis amusingly picks a nice view and pan-
tomimes digging a hole and wiping with a pinecone or a rock.
Then he tells us that under no circumstances are we allowed
to bring toilet paper along with us. He says he's going to sort
through our personal possessions, too, to make sure we aren't
carrying any other contraband—drugs, cigarettes, hair gel. I'm
suddenly feeling less like a midcareer professional than a juvenile
delinquent. There is no way a thirty-two-year-old guy is going to
paw through my stuff or tell me I'm not going to use toilet paper.
I'm a grown-up, I respect the wilderness, and I'll gladly pack out
what I pack in, I tell him pleasantly, with a look that says he can
go fuck himself if he disagrees. Tina grabs her package of Wet
Wipes in solidarity and stuffs it back into her pack. I give her a
big, warm smile.

We load up our packs with what seems to be a huge amount
of food, along with tents, ropes, first aid kits, and helmets. The
packs are too heavy for any of us to put on without help, and we
stagger to the top of the trail. As we begin to descend from the
pine trees to the pink rocky canyon, I try to let go of my grumpy
resistance: I have to be with these people for a week and should
make the best of it. We stop to learn how to read a topographical
map with a compass, something my dad taught me three decades
ago, and then inexplicably head toward a place on that map that
doesn't have a trail or water. But I don't argue the route. When
Dennis transfers some of the weight from a lighter, weaker woman's pack to mine, I don't complain. I have more experience in the
wilderness than any of the other participants, and I'm stronger
than the other women, so I'll shoulder more of the load.

We bushwhack our way to a campsite, brambles scratching
our arms, legs trembling with each heavy step. Soon a couple of
the women are crying from the exertion. I'm annoyed that we've
left a perfectly nice and pretty trail to savage our way through
a prickly gulley where no human should ever venture, but I'm
determined to be cheerful because if someone isn't cheerful—
especially me—things are bound to get really ugly.

When we finally reach the campsite, a sloping piece of scrabbly
ground, we're exhausted. I go into action, firing up the stove, since
I'm the only one who knows how to do it except Dennis, whose
only advice is to learn to survive in the wilderness already. I'm in-
wardly cranky at the others for bursting into tears and kvetching
about their packs and realize I'm missing a good party in the city
tonight. Maybe it wasn't such a good idea to come. I'm not sure
when I got derailed from that yoga spa idea, doing morning sun
salutations on a mountaintop, followed by water aerobics, deep-
tissue massage, flirting with fit eco entrepreneurs over organic cuisine, and slipping into high-thread-count sheets at night.

Gretchen, the pale young recent college graduate, is watching
me assemble a wind barrier, pump the gas, and light the stove,
and she asks me how it works. We are all tired and hungry, and it
would be a hell of a lot easier if I just did it myself, and how could
she have signed up for Outward Bound without ever having lit
a camp stove anyway? That's like driving a car without knowing how to change a flat tire, nothing my dad would've ever let
any of us do. I wipe my face with my bandanna and realize I'm
sounding a lot like my *über*-competent dad, here in my brain, and
one of the reasons Mom went on Outward Bound was so that she

could learn to light the damn camp stove herself. I turn the stove off, disassemble it, and hand it to Gretchen. I explain it to her step by step, rubbing my mittens together to stay warm, and when she finally lights it and puts a pot of water on to boil, she's thrilled and gives me a big hug.

Tina is still sniffling and counting the scratches on her arms when Gretchen and I pour a package of powdered potato soup into the boiling water, which turns the soup bright blue. Tina looks at the soup, the strangest thing, and her tears dissolve into laughter, which makes her tears flow faster. When Bob tells her, "You said you came here to cry," she laughs even harder. After our neon blue dinner (someone remembers an elementary school experiment where iodine, which we used to purify the spring water, turns potato starch blue), Tina rubs my shoulders for having wrangled the stove, and I relax a little. At least I'm getting a massage.

It strikes me, as she digs deep into my shoulders, that Tina, Gretchen, and the other women here need an experience like Outward Bound to tap their inner reserves of strength, just as my mother had. They need the confidence that follows overcoming a tough challenge. My parents, on the other hand, raised me to carry a pack in the wilderness without complaining and to be competent in the outdoors and everywhere else. I spent a good part of my childhood playing the home version of Outward Bound. As a result, I've never been able to use the charming helpless card with men, to let them feel heroic or even useful, because I can manage almost anything perfectly well on my own. I'm sure I intimidate a lot of men with my competence, and I'm tired, among some women, of always being the strong and reliable one (which in my twenties tended to attract some really crazy friends, who always needed to be rescued; it took me years to realize that not only were they draining me, those energy vampires, but that only they could rescue themselves). The last thing I need right now is an experience that's supposed to teach me to be tougher and more independent, developing my I-can-do-that-myself spirit. I have a strong suspicion, in fact, that those are the very qualities that will be the least helpful in getting me out of my private wilderness.

It's easy for me to be a leader in an Outward Bound group. What's harder is to sit back, let other people make mistakes and figure things out, and be patient while they stumble along. I probably need to spend this week in the outdoors more or less doing the opposite of what everyone else is doing, letting go of responsibility, resisting the urge to do everything myself, bringing up the rear on the trail. While I'm at it, I need not waste the entire time we're hiking composing letters in my head to Outward Bound International about how the wilderness shouldn't be difficult for the sake of difficulty, personal growth need not be puritanically punitive, and four plastic honey bears are way too many for seven adults to carry for a five-day trip. I'm going to have to make this my own Inward Bound and quietly work on being as patient and gentle as you can be with a seventy-five-pound pack on your back.

At dusk we manage to pitch our tents, fluff up our sleeping bags, and, stomping to keep warm, watch the sun set in a pink-streaked sky behind the hoodoo rocks.

On the third day, over instant coffee and oatmeal, we prepare to split up to do a twenty-four-hour solo, a full day alone, which makes everyone else in the group anxious. We go around the circle again to talk about our fears, and while others voice their nervousness about wild animals and freaking out with their feelings, I am silently gleeful to finally get a chance to be off by myself.

Dennis leads each of us to a different spot, where we can't see one another and from which we aren't supposed to move more than ten feet in the next twenty-four hours. We're allowed to bring along only water and trail mix (despite the vast quantities of food we're schlepping, fasting is supposed to help with reflection) and a journal to write our thoughts. The minute Dennis leaves, I eat all my trail mix, explore my little spot—a slick rock tucked under an overhang—and then read the fine print on my medicine bottles. After five minutes, I have nothing left to do. Now I'm supposed to think about the big picture of my life. I dig into my pack, unroll a pair of socks, and smoke the joint I hid inside.

I eye the boundaries of my spot, which seems to be shrinking. I can't sit still in one little place for twenty-four hours, so I immediately get up and move. I walk beyond the edge—what the hell, I can take care of myself—and for the next several hours explore rock formations farther and farther away from where I'm supposed to be. This is what I came to Canyonlands for: I love the feeling of the smooth rock under my hands, the dance of shifting weight as I make my way up some boulders, the concentration of figuring out where to place my hands and feet, the feeling of muscles I rarely use. I know the rules of the wilderness: I'm careful to check for rattlesnakes before I place my hands under any ledges, and I don't climb any higher than I'm willing to fall. When I finally return to my spot, I still have many hours until sunset. You forget how long days are.

Physically spent, I sip some water, deeply regret that I ate all my trail mix already, decide against trying to sneak back to my backpack for some banana chips, and lie back in the shade to take a little nap.

I think about my mother's Outward Bound trip and the journal she wrote while she was on her own solo, which she shared with me. She never mentioned her family in those pages, which made me feel odd. Instead, she wrote about her group of lively and strong women and about the pleasurable freedom she felt when they all splashed naked in a river to get clean after a tough hike. I suppose it was the first time in twenty years we four kids had been out of Mom's thoughts, the first time she felt really free to be herself.

It was even more surprising to read the magazine article that came out after the trip, the way the writer described my mother: "Ginny, at 46, has never journeyed away from her husband and children for more than a few days." It made her sound uncharacteristically timid. The trip was in 1974, during the throes of the women's movement, and the women in the group were eager to explore who else they could be away from their families—and the writer, perhaps, to exaggerate the theme.

I recall my mother, though, as always being far more adventuresome than the rest of the moms in our suburban neighborhood. In those days, whatever encouraged pleasant, stay-at-home casserole making among most of Littleton's wives seemed to have an opposite effect on my mom. A fairly recent convert to the

Democratic Party, she threw herself into the civil rights, antiwar, feminist, and environmental movements with the zeal of the newly religious, participating to whatever extent she could between grocery shopping, making Sloppy Joes, and going to parent-teacher conferences. Over the course of the sixties she'd changed out of Jackie O. shift dresses, poufy hairdos, and ladylike pumps into bell-bottomed jeans, denim shirts with appliquéd sunflowers, and hiking boots (once, in a restroom at the Four Corners National Monument, a woman in the stall next to Mom noticed those boots and ran out screaming, convinced there was a man inside). Dad was a good sport about all of this, considering himself lucky to have married someone who was willing to go to Yellowstone on their honeymoon, working in the dining room while he was out being a fishing guide. He liked coming home to dinner on the table but otherwise encouraged Mom to do whatever made her happy, which eventually involved a lot of exploration beyond her own little spot.

When I was five, Mom sat me down on the lawn and told me that she wanted me to be "more independent" than my three older sisters. When she explained what that big word meant, I was all for the idea. As part of this new independence deal, she said she would not be my room mother in kindergarten, as she had for my sisters, bringing cookies and supervising crafts in class. The trade-off was that I got to go along with Mom when she was out finding interesting pursuits closer to home. When she heard that Realtors in our neighborhood wouldn't sell houses to African American families, for instance, she got involved in the fair housing movement and took me to demonstrations, meetings, and trials. I missed some school, but our outings are the only memories I can call up from my year in kindergarten. On one occasion, I'm told, we met Dr. Martin Luther King, Jr., though all I remember is being downtown, holding hands, and singing "Kumbaya" in a circle with a great number of people, many of whom, unlike the people in Littleton, were black. That was a thrilling alternative to a day at South Elementary School, and it became clear early on that going places away from home was far more interesting than staying put, which was my mom's view of things, too.

That's why, not long after, Mom decided to hop a freight train across Colorado. As a physician's wife and stay-at-home mother, she said she needed more excitement in her forties and vowed to take more risks in her life. When a couple of younger, footloose friends called with this zany idea, she couldn't refuse. I begged her to go along, probably reminding her that she hadn't been my room mother in kindergarten and that I was doing a very good job of being independent, but she said riding freight trains was only for big girls. Secretly, she remembers, she hoped my father would insist that no wife of his was going to hop a damned freight train. Instead, appreciating the romance and outdoorsy spirit of it all, he offered to drive her to the station.

At the freight yards, my mother, who hadn't grasped the nuances of hobo behavior, politely asked a railroad man which train was bound for Grand Junction, as if she had a first-class ticket tucked inside her purse. "That one," he snarled at her, "and don't let me see you." She and the others jumped aboard and watched miles of wide-open western landscape roll by. After a few days, my mother hitchhiked home, but her appetite for adventure hadn't been satisfied, only whetted. She signed up for graduate school, went to Vietnam War protests, took a horseback trek through the Wyoming Tetons, rode bicycles in Europe, and took us all to Mexico for the summer. The Outward Bound trip seemed to be just another of her many excursions out of the house and into the world. Sometimes my sisters wondered why she wouldn't just play tennis or join the garden club like the other mothers.

But she couldn't help it; she got her restless spirit from my grandmother, who had an adventurous streak of her own. Grandma's husband left her when she was pregnant with my mother—running off to Mexico with a redhead for a quickie divorce—and she raised her child alone, on a teacher's salary, during the Great Depression. But in the summer she'd pack up the two of them and explore the West, sleeping wherever they landed when night fell—a Navajo chicken yard, a desert gulch, a mountain ghost town. They'd pull out the portable stove and eat pancakes at every meal. "It never occurred to me that we were poor," my mother says. Between trips, they lived in a Cape Cod–style house in Cleveland Heights, with mom's grandmother and a maiden Aunt Belle, who gave piano lessons, drinking tea in delicate Haviland china cups and speaking in subdued voices. My doted-upon mother, the only child in the vicinity, stayed within the confines of the house and of proper manners, which surely contributed to her lifelong desire to break away.

Somehow, the Outward Bound trip gave my mother more confidence than her other adventures. Despite the fact that she liked to hike and camp, Mom had never really had to rely on herself in the outdoors. "Dad always took care of everything," she says. He set up the gear and built the fire, and at the end of the day, Mom was still the one making dinner for everyone, even if it was on tin plates, and washing up afterward. He scouted ahead while she held my hand, the youngest and slowest, pulling me up the trail.

On the Outward Bound course, Mom's patrol camped on the snow, pitched their own tents, rappelled down rock faces, backpacked dozens of miles, and climbed a pink desert mountain in the snow, appropriately named "Fern's Nipple." The magazine writer described the biggest challenge: climbing a steep, smooth rock face, with my mother on the ropes behind her. "When I finally see her face, it is transformed: a battle photo—a face under siege . . . she flops beside me, bursting into tears." My mother remembers that crying. "It gave us an incredible sense of euphoria to accomplish something that difficult."

Later she said that the course had given her some of the grit she needed to face a working world that was still, in 1975, fairly hostile to women. It helped steel her for the transition from being a stay-at-home mom to a part-time adviser at an alternative college and then a full-time nursing home residents' advocate for twenty years, becoming a nationally respected and beloved figure in that field, inducted into the Colorado Women's Hall of Fame, and, thirty-five years after her work in the civil rights movement, presented with the state's Martin Luther King, Jr., humanitarian award. She shelved that plaque in the garage with a pile of others, next to a backpack she never wanted to throw away.

In some ways, having the freedom to pursue a career after kids, not to mention far-flung outdoor adventures, my mother

did eventually manage to have it all. I'm proud of her and grateful for her spirit, but I sometimes wonder if I'm paying a price
for identifying so closely with her desire for independence. Now
that I'm forty, I feel a vague sense of defeat, as if I've done everything backward, starting with a career, leaving no time for a
family. What to do next is completely up in the air. All the un-
complaining toughness and competence I learned as a kid, along
with my mile-wide independent streak, may have served me well
in the wilderness, at school, and at work and has gotten me a lot
of things my mother yearned for—an interesting career, spontaneous travel, varied friends. But it hasn't done much for my intimate relationships.

My mother has always had my father to fall back on, to saddle
her horse and dust her off when she got home. My parents have
been married for about fifty years, and though they've had some
bumps along the way, they are best friends, still make each other
laugh, and are impossible to imagine apart.

I, on the other hand, have no man in my life to say, "Go ahead,
honey, be independent, it's adorable."

IN THE EARLY morning, the sandstone glowing pink from the
brand-new sun, I pull out my notebook. Normally, I love to sit
and write, especially in front of a stunning landscape. But since
Dennis told me I *had* to write and to make it meaningful, I can't
put down a word. That undoubtedly says something about me
that would be worth writing about in itself, but I just can't. It's
pretty here in this canyon, but it isn't the momentous experience
it was for my mother, and my stomach is grumbling.

So I sit in my spot and come up with nothing. Bored, I finally write a list, as far as I can remember, of all the men I've slept with. I put a star by the one-night stands, of which there are disconcertingly many, but at least not in the last few years. That has to be personal growth. There was a decade in there where there were only three men, my period of long-term serial monogamous relationships, two with wonderful guys I'm still friendly with—my grand-ex and my great-grand-ex, as I call them—the third being my ex-husband, with whom I am not. After my divorce, I see, the list goes haywire again.

Along with being hungry, this list isn't doing anything for my mood on this otherwise rosy morning. Why have I been so spectacularly unsuccessful with men, in the long term, especially since my marriage ended? Apart from my sweet and scrumptious rendezvous with the Professor, things have been disappointing and unsubstantial in the romance category. I can't remember when someone unrelated by blood told me he loved me, much less the last time I dug my fingernails into the side of the mattress, tossed my hair back, and let loose a cry underneath a happy, energetic, sweaty man. Okay, I'm forty, but that's not so old, and though I could stand to lose a few pounds, one good thing about being forty is that you finally realize that fat is a lot more in your head than in the minds of most men. I can't fathom what the problem is all about. God knows I have tried to find a relationship, going on dates, writing hopefully witty online profiles, suffering through coffee with men who recite a litany of achievements or bad past relationships, my hopes continually raised and dashed, attracting dull or disastrous men and even one dangerous creep, being appraised and found wanting, suspecting I'm too independent, neurotic, oversensitive, smart, talkative, reserved, tough, edgy, whatever. Who knows. There is no explanation, no reasonable rationale for the vast chasm between my friends, who find me lovable, funny, generous, and warm—if occasionally difficult—and men who guzzle down one Sauvignon Blanc and head for the hills. At a certain point all you can do is laugh.

Dennis twitters like a bird to collect us for breakfast, and we gather back on a big smooth rock in a circle. I'm surprised at how glad I am to see these people and give everyone a big hug. Over heaping bowls of granola and powdered milk, everyone reads what he or she has written. I'm quite moved at how Tina describes losing her friend, saying this challenge of being in the wilderness is making her feel like herself again. The Realtor does a sensitive postmortem on her last relationship. Gretchen is delighted with herself for making it through the solo, and she seems visibly stronger. Even the CEO of the institutional food company is sweet and self-revealing. I'm the last one to speak, and everyone looks at me expectantly, but I don't want to share what I've written. No way.

"But you're a *writer*," the venture capitalist insists. I shake my head no, embarrassed. Dennis insists that I *have* to read, since I'm part of the group. So I pull out my piece of paper: "Daniel, Josh, the film major guy, Kent, the short guy from Psi U, Eric . . ." The group is silent.

Then at last Tina laughs a little. "That's it? A list? We're spilling our guts here, and you came up with a *list*?"

I shrug and mumble something about not being able to muster up anything else.

"Okay, well, there must be some reason you wrote the list," says the Realtor. "You must have been thinking about your relationships or something. Why don't you tell us about what was going on in your head?"

"I don't know," I say, furiously stirring my instant coffee. I'm on the spot and have to come up with something. So I tell them I was just thinking about the crazy string of guys I've been with, marveling at what ridiculous situations I get myself into.

"Such as?" Tina asks.

The men in the group start examining their spoons and the ants on the rock.

I start telling them about how I can't seem to meet the right guy, how somehow I end up on spectacularly bad dates. I laugh. "Just bad luck, I guess." Tina and the Realtor nod along, they know about bad dates. Tina raises her eyebrows, waiting to hear more. Encouraged and wanting to lighten the mood and shift attention away from me and how I feel about my list, which is not so great, I launch into stories about my most disastrous dates. There was the guy who pulled over on the side of the road and told me his ex-wife had a temporary restraining order against him and he'd spent time in Atascadero—not a nice hotel in Carmel, ha ha, but the California facility for the criminally insane. And the chef who got so drunk he actually left skid marks on my couch. In the midst of telling these stories, which always vastly amuse my friends—the worse the date, the better, as far as the retelling is concerned—I pause and see that no one in this group, not even Tina, is laughing. They're digging around in their oatmeal as if there's gold hidden in there.

I wipe my eyes, look around at the landscape, and comment on how lovely the sky is this morning. Gretchen puts an arm around my shoulders briefly, and then we do the dishes.

For the last two days, we explore the canyons with only a day pack, feeling light as lizards as we scramble on rocks in the sun. We jump into cool sandstone pools and find a shady arch to nap under. The final night, after hiking fifteen miles, we ascend a 1,000-foot mesa in the dark. We manage it slowly, giving helping hands, taking breaks. I find a wellspring of strength in myself, not in climbing the mountain but in patiently encouraging the slowest hiker from behind, singing Aretha Franklin and punk-rock songs to keep her spirits up for the last grueling hour. When we finally reach the top of the mesa at midnight, we throw down our sleeping bags and sleep huddled together in the wind.

The trip ends up having some lasting effects on the group. Gretchen, the timid college grad, having hiked her way through some self-esteem issues, goes to New York City for a master's degree, loses weight, and transforms into a chic, pale-skinned intellectual. The socks manager quits smoking for good and gets involved in an Audubon program, making a bunch of new friends. The skinny Realtor finds a rich new boyfriend and gains a few pounds. The institutional food manager buys a vacation home and retires part-time, spending more time with his grand-child. The computer guy gets a new job and a girlfriend. Dennis and the venture capitalist break up with their respective partners, take a trip around the world together, and get married, inviting us all to come play paintball at their wedding, which I do not attend. I have an X-ray taken of my spine; the seventy-five-pound pack has compressed two discs, apparently permanently, and my doctor tells me I can never backpack again and that I should take up yoga.

On the bus ride back to the motel, I'm not sure what this trip has accomplished for me. It's has gotten me out of the house and into the wide wilderness; it's distracted me a bit, but I haven't managed to venture very far into my internal landscape. I'm not sure I feel any better about my situation than when I set out. I suspect that when I get home I'm just going to want to pick up and leave again.

As we ride the bus back from the wilderness to the motel for a shower, we pass the turnoff to a campground in Canyonlands National Park, where my parents are, coincidentally, vacationing this weekend. At seventy-four, my mother, who has been diagnosed with Parkinson's disease, is no longer backpacking, but she still sets out with my dad to find the scenery they love. I hope that when I'm her age, I will be as willing to get outside and as content to sit in the sun, accepting my limitations, contemplating the canyons. I admire that toughness in her, and that softness.

Chapter Three

MIDDLETOWN,
CONNECTICUT *
NEW YORK CITY

2002

June is lush and leafy in the Connecticut countryside, moistly warm and smelling like summer the way San Francisco never does. The minute I arrive at Wesleyan University in Middletown, I want to take off my shoes and run down a grassy hill. I want to dance outdoors to African drums, eat a steamed cheeseburger at a diner, thumb through random books in the library stacks, and walk around the cemetery drinking beer from a brown paper bag, reading old tombstone inscriptions. I want to be my college self for a while, with everything to look forward to, every possibility spread out before me, like a fat catalogue of classes.

I'm here for my twentieth college reunion and wander around the stately campus, with its ivy and dark red bricks, 1970s-era dorms, and modern concrete arts center, which, though familiar, seems as foreign a landscape as when I first arrived from Colorado. I came here as a chubby seventeen-year-old from Littleton, wearing a blouse I'd sewn in home ec class with little pink flowers sprinkled on a western yoke, and spent most of my first year trying too hard to catch up with the fast company, prep school kids and punk-rock New Yorkers. I had wanted to go far from Colorado, to have a completely different experience, but I'd had no idea just how far away it would be.

Now the recent graduates all look as if they're about fifteen, wearing private galleries of tattoos, taking themselves very seriously, gesticulating while they speak. I remember being that earnest, drinking too many cups of coffee too late at night, smoking clove cigarettes, arguing about something very important and abstract, no doubt related to feminism, such as whether we're all eventually headed toward androgyny or if you have to be a lesbian to really be a feminist (I remember announcing to my mother that I was a "theoretical lesbian" who just preferred sleeping with men, which didn't much alarm her). I felt that my brain was on fire in those days, and only constant conversation and massive amounts of reading—along with a few hits of pot—would keep it stoked.

Crossing the campus, I run across bald-headed dads and weary-looking moms who capably keep half an eye on their children while talking animatedly to other moms, women they haven't seen since senior year. It takes me a while to realize that these nearly middle-aged people are from my class, i.e., my age. Everywhere are tidy groups of alumni in summer outfits, khakis with webbed belts, white sweaters slung around tanned shoulders. I half expected everyone to be wearing the same jeans, T-shirts, and flip-flops they wore the day after graduation, to have untamed hair and skinny midriffs, looking as if they just stepped out of dance class. Instead, they look so grown-up and responsible, so purposeful and prosperous, so paired off.

Seeing them, I feel as if I've truly arrived in the heart of the strange territory that is forty and hope these people, who seem to have figured it all out, will give me some clues. I'm among my peers, who had similar opportunities and went to the same freshman orientation but who look so much more settled than I am. Forty doesn't appear to be so foreign to them: their lives are full of milestones—jobs, marriages, moves, birth announcements, kindergarten, grammar school—that have clearly marked the path along the way. They look satisfied and well tended, exuding a quiet air of accomplishment (though here in academia I have to remind myself that reunion attendees suffer from selection bias— no one who has made a real mess of his life shows up).

For the most part, it's an air they've earned; I know because for years I have been the class secretary and recorded every award, entrepreneurial success, artistic achievement, or PhD my fellow classmates have amassed. It is an impressive group, full of creative thinkers, scientists, and humanitarians. They are people I am proud to know; some of my richest and most enduring friendships began here. The cliché about Wesleyan was always that the student population was "diverse," and they have indeed proven themselves to be a group of individuals with singular talents. They are always writing in, apologizing for their slight contributions to the notes, saying they've done nothing recently but open a low-income mental health center or taken a little theater piece to Broadway or become the CEO of a Fortune 500 company.

Over the past decade, though, much of the news they've sent in has been announcing their marriages, and then, en suite, their children. I probably report these domestic events with less enthusiasm than other class secretaries do. Even in this unconventional

group, it seems like a failure to have not been able to be both cre-
atively successful and effortlessly accomplish the conventional
spouse and kids.

I suppose if I'd wanted to have a lifetime partner, someone I
could rely on, I should have looked around more carefully when
I was in college; by far the highest-quality pool of men I've ever
splashed around with were the ones I met in Middletown. Plus, it
seems that meeting someone early on, practically growing up together, is the secret to a lasting relationship: after fifty-five years,
my parents still laugh at each other's jokes. Kristin, a dear friend
since we were ten, is happy with the guy she met working in a
pizzeria during college. My oldest sister, Cindy, met her husband,
Brad, when they were fourteen; after thirty years, they hug each
other with tears in their eyes if they've been apart for more than
three days. Those couples are like overlapping circles in a Venn
diagram, with a lot more in common in the middle than on the
sides. They're hard acts to follow.

Not that I should've married one of those glorious Wesleyan
guys right after graduation—I had too much of the world to experience, not to mention too many interesting men to meet. But
at the time, I was more intent on competing with the men I found
interesting than eventually marrying one of them, which may
have been an unfortunate ripple effect of seventies-era feminism,
or just bad timing.

Someone waves at me; I recognize the couple, and greet
and hug them. One of the advantages of being class secretary,
twenty years later, is that everyone knows you. You're retroac-
tively popular.

They tell me I look good and heard I had a book out, so at least I'm passing in this crowd, not obviously someone who is still living in the same apartment she rented in the hippie Haight Ashbury a year after she graduated, someone who could barely buy the plane ticket to the reunion, much less make a sizable contribution to the alumni fund. (Despite all my women's studies classes, I never paid much attention to making real money, always assuming I'd marry someone who'd bring home the bacon while I'd write witty essays about why I stopped being a vegetarian.) I'm staying in a dorm room, not a hotel, which seems to concretize—to use a very Wesleyan word—the fact that I haven't quite made it into successful adulthood. But perhaps because I've recorded all my classmates' accomplishments, I'm more keenly aware of them. Maybe everyone feels like I do when reading the class notes, the way you feel fat and frumpy after browsing through a copy of *Vogue*.

The undercurrent of insecurity persists at the cocktail hour, as I casually listen to what my classmates are up to—where they live and where they summer, where they send their kids to school. Part of me realizes, as I eventually realized twenty years ago, that much of that cool confidence is an illusion. When I finally have a few real conversations with my classmates, it becomes clear that several of them have lives that are as messy and uncertain as mine—a divorced social worker with two kids, an environmentalist struggling to make a business out of his ideals, an artist who hates selling real estate to get by, a heartsick dad whose wife just left him and took along the kids they adopted.

The ones who seem the most successful at second glance are

the ones who seem to have figured out, with some equanimity, that midlife is never all you expected it would be, especially when your college years were so bright, but getting older brings a few satisfactions of its own. Instead of comforting me, this just adds to the list of things I've failed at: marriage, having children, making money, and now, having a mature perspective about it all.

As the evening wears on, it strikes me that while most of the men are as clever and confident as they were in college, full of ironic observations and witty word play, several of the women seem to have sipped some of the same punch I did that gives you a sneaking suspicion that you're a disappointment at forty, that things haven't turned out the way you might have hoped.

I run into Kate, with her mesmerizing blue eyes, who was a brilliant actress in college, talking with Chloe, who manages to run an environmental nonprofit while raising three children. Chloe asks Kate if she's still acting, and Kate shrugs it off. "Not with the kids." She seems content, but as she moves on to greet someone else, I ask Chloe if she thinks that deep down, Kate is genuinely happy exploring other talents—or whether she's acting.

"Hard to say," says Chloe, as we watch Kate sparkling in the center of another little group. Chloe shakes her head. "Everyone was in love with her in college."

"And with you," I say.

Chloe laughs and Ellen comes up, someone I envied for her effortless beauty and long-term boyfriend, whom she married after college. She was fun: we traipsed around a carnival doing interviews with the hard-living carnies to make a documentary for film class and once secretly drank bottles from our birth year from her parents' stash (since she's a few months older than me, we had to pop open both the '60 and '61 Bordeaux, a first experience with French wine that definitely beat my first experience with sex). She and her boyfriend were both talented writers. Now she tells me she's read my book and marvels that I have done so well in my career, getting so much published. "You have such a great life," she says, almost wistfully, "traveling all over the world and writing about it."

"It's true," says Chloe. "The farthest we ever travel is to Long Island."

This makes me uncomfortable, because while I'm grateful that I've had adventures, I'm also thinking that *they* have such great lives, with their smart husbands and adorable kids and ability to work part-time. It's not that the grass is greener, it's that you can never be on both sides of the lawn at the same time. Ellen tells us an idea for an article and asks if I think she could get it published in a women's magazine. Of course, I say, that's a piece of cake for someone like you. I can't fathom why she sounds so uncertain. She sighs. "It's been hard for me to get back into that world, I've been so busy with the kids," she says. "I don't know where to start."

Ellen waves at a friend across the room, kisses us good-bye, and Chloe whispers that Ellen's husband is at the top of the media food chain—almost as if, by some necessity of gender physics, their careers had to go in opposite directions.

Susan taps me on the shoulder and pulls me away from Chloe. Like me, she's working on her second or third gin and tonic. I

used to marvel at Susan for being able to discuss *Capitalist Patri-
archy and the Case for Socialist Feminism* during the day and then
go off and capably flirt with guys at frat parties. She had been
fiercely optimistic that we could have it all, sure that we would
be free and creative and sexy and self-actualized, all while raising
kids, sharing the chores, and making a lot of money. Now she's a
lawyer with a big corporation, single, and not dating anyone. "It
sucks," she says, taking a long sip of her drink. "I work too hard. I
never have time to meet anyone." I nod along as she tells me how
she stays late at the office, later even than the men who go home
to their families, since she has no excuse to go home early at all.
She finishes her drink, turns her head for a moment, then flashes
a smile as big and bright as the diamond on her right hand. "But
I've made partner."

"Congratulations," I say. "I'll have to put that in the class
notes."

As we leave the cocktail party, I picture these extraordinary
women from my class, loading up their minivans or catching
planes, scattering across the country. Most have made uneasy
choices in the intervening years. Certainly they're coping and
taking great pleasure in parts of their lives, but many feel like
something is missing. They are exhausted. They are frantic to finally get pregnant, and some are having fertility problems. They
aren't passionate about their work but want to be. They love their
spouses and kids, of course, but either they want more in their
lives or they're overwhelmed with too much. Or, like me, they're
single and doing satisfying work but dogged with a vague sense
of defeat about their relationships.

I walk across the campus lawn to dinner with Barbara, a psychologist, who has been in love and married twice since we were in school, one union ending in tragedy. She has always been soulful and perceptive. I make some crack about the singles table at dinner, and though we haven't seen each other in a decade, she sees right through me. "I know you're sad about being single," she says. Happily, she doesn't try to diagnose the problem, or give me any pat advice about how I ought to learn to be more open to a relationship, make a list of all the qualities I want in a man and visualize him arriving at my doorstep, or put pink candles on my bedroom windowsill to attract him with feng shui. "Enjoy being single while it lasts," she says, letting me in on the secret that being married and having children isn't all I romanticize it to be. There are plenty of days when she'd like to be single just for a few hours, not to mention have a sexy fling with a man on an Italian island. Not that she would trade it all, not for the world.

"We can't have it all," I say, trying out some of that mature perspective.

"Maybe we can't have it all at once," she says. "But there are phases in life; maybe we can have it all, just one thing after another, serially."

"You think?"

"It's like the Manhattan trifecta," she says. I raise my eyebrows; she's from New York, and I have no idea what she's talking about. "In Manhattan, it's impossible to get the great relationship, the great job, and the great apartment all at once," she says.

I smile. "I do have a great job and a great apartment."

"Then if the right man comes along, you'd better be careful about your lease."

I laugh and give her a hug. Maybe the right guy will come along, although I realize that two decades after college, you have to expect that everyone you meet will have difficult traits, awkward histories, and annoying habits (I know I do). In any case, looking around at my classmates seated so smartly at the white linen tables set up on the lawn, I still have twinges of regret that I didn't eventually marry one of these amazing college men, these funny, high-SAT-scoring guys who were always asking thoughtful questions and called themselves feminists not just so they could get laid but because they honestly respected women.

But you can't second-guess history. During dinner, an accomplished and engaging guy comes up to me while I'm in line for a drink and confesses, tipsy, that he once had a huge crush on me. I'm flattered and floored. "That," I finally muster, "is a painful thing to hear from such an attractive, married man." I find myself fantasizing about the men at the reunion—How did I overlook this wonderful guy? Why can't we run off together now and try again?—but most are married; and not only are there rules about married men, there are delusions, on both sides, about still-single women they may have gazed at in government class or smooched and never slept with decades ago.

After dinner, I walk back to my dorm room, which is in the same complex of buildings where I lived as a sophomore, the year I had the most trouble with men, food, sex, pot, paranoia, personal style, and everything but my classes, whose challenges I could at least work through if I tried hard enough.

I brush my hair and freshen up for the party that starts later on, then stop at my reflection in the mirror. Here I am, with my prospects for finding a mate heading steadily downhill on the graph of time, and I suddenly look older and fatter, with wiggly arms and creases on my face like I've slept wrong. I have never been full-on beautiful, so losing my looks isn't going to be as hard for me as for someone who always relied more heavily on her physical charms. But still.

As I stare in the mirror, I remember another party and another black dress, slinky with spaghetti straps. It was sophomore year and I was unhappy with how I looked. "You're beautiful," a woman next to me said to my reflection. "Just forget about it." That moment, with my protruding collarbones, tiny waist, smooth skin, and long blond hair, was probably when I looked my most conventionally attractive. But I got there by extreme dieting and purging (I thought I'd invented bulimia) and felt anything but beautiful inside. There were so many pressures on me—thrown into a situation where I thought I had to be thin, witty, East Coast–smart, sexually experienced, invulnerable—that something had to give, and it ended up being my self-esteem, along with my lunch. The campus therapist asked why I couldn't just control myself—this being the Dark Ages in the history of eating disorders—and I told him that that was exactly the fucking problem. So many of us young women could have earned PhDs in eating issues, or in anything else, for all the time we wasted on our unhappy relationships with food and our bodies. Not to mention how much joyful eating and delicious sex we missed out on.

Thank God those days and issues are out of the way. I look in the mirror, apply some bright lipstick, pat my belly, and decide there's no way I'm going to waste any more of my evening with my sophomore self, who barely had a sense of humor (one of the things that definitely improves with age). I'm taking my forty-one-year-old ass back out to a party.

The alumni fete is at one of the old fraternity houses, which smells faintly like twenty-year-old beer. A band is playing New Wave cover songs from the late seventies and early eighties, the Talking Heads and the Clash, which we all simultaneously enjoy and dimly, uncomfortably realize that the band is playing as oldies.

No matter. In the living room, on worn wooden floors, a group of us dance, warming up slowly, then moving and shaking through the strata of our bodies to an energetic, euphoric 1982. I am back in the body of the young woman who, no matter how confused she was about what it meant to be a feminist woman making her way in the world, could dance her way down to a truth, holding and expressing rhythm in every part of her being in a way that was completely, unabashedly female. Dancing kept me grounded in college and transformed me from a brain with a ponytail, supported by undifferentiated mass, into someone who inhabited her body with flexible, energetic assurance.

Just a few hours a week of dance class with a warm, exuberant, and challenging professor changed my body image: when we watched a videotape of ourselves leaping across the room, I wondered who that graceful woman was wearing the same color leotard I always wore. The subtler lessons of dance class were harder to learn, such as the idea that in order to improvise with someone else you have to really listen to them, to respond rather than react, a notion that has tickled my brain ever since but which I've rarely managed to embody.

I dance with these people I danced with so long ago, with no judgments, just joy. It reminds me of sunny days in spring when we'd dance in a circle to African drums, feeling ecstatic and tribal there in Connecticut, unleashing our bodies, passion, and energy. "That was better than sex," I recall one guy remarking when the dancing stopped, and we all lay back on the grass, sweaty and spent.

AFTER THE REUNION, my head buzzing, I head to New York City for a few days, a city I love and lived in briefly during college, doing a magazine internship (I was Xeroxing for cokeheads at *Rolling Stone;* the only time an editor spoke to me except to give me shitwork was to ask, "Why is it all the women who work here are pears?" I was still too young and cowed by New York magazine editors to come back with a proper reply, which I'm still practicing in my head). I returned the summer after graduation, because it seemed like the place a real writer ought to live, even if it meant working three part-time gigs that were only distantly related to journalism and moving from one illegal sublet to another. New York was a feast, though—for art, cheap ethnic food, used bookstores, dance classes, and wonderfully complicated friends.

I left the city around the time I was offered my first full-time job in publishing, as an assistant on the advertising side of *Omni* magazine, owned by *Penthouse,* where you had to look at soft-core porn covers every time you stepped out of the elevator. I considered the offer, because it was a job, and you have to start somewhere, especially if you have no contacts in New York, nor a trust fund, but it seemed to define soullessness. I'd have to put on an *outfit* every day, would come home too tired to write, never see the outdoors à la Colorado, and would face the distinct danger of turning into a bitch.

Just then my late Grandma intervened, leaving me that small inheritance, and I went for breakfast at the Greek diner near my apartment to mull things over. Before the waiter even poured the weak coffee, I decided New York City could live without me and I was leaving for Greece. (Who knows what would've happened if I'd been in a Chinese restaurant.) I spent the rest of the summer temping for an ad agency, which tried to hire me after I took advantage of a break from word processing to test their client's new coconut liqueur, creating several new cocktails and marketing ideas just so I didn't have to go back to typing. But I couldn't see working somewhere you could get fired for drinking a Diet Coke if they shilled for Pepsi.

Nine months in the Mediterranean put to rights everything that had troubled me at Wesleyan or in New York. It awakened all my slumbering senses: I had my first fig from a tree in Greece, my first fat black olive in Spain, and my first simultaneous orgasm in Israel. I learned to dance flamenco and ride a camel, I saw the art I'd seen only on slides at Wesleyan, and I kept a journal along the way. When I returned to New York, I sensed right away that it was too confining a space; I needed some cross between the city's culture and Colorado's outdoors, and set out, on a hunch, to San Francisco. I cried as I crossed the Golden Gate Bridge and have felt at home ever since.

But I still get a thrill every time I visit New York. Part of it is peeking in on a parallel life that I passed on; part of it is feeding on its energy and unexpected scenes. This time, it happens that Doug, a childhood friend who is a film director, has a movie opening. In line for the movie, before heading in, Doug introduces me to Gustavo, a friend of his who is standing next to me. Also in the film business, Gustavo has shaggy black hair and is wearing a mountain parka and hiking boots in New York City, oblivious to fashion. He has a soft accent I can place only in the vicinity of Latin America. I have a soft spot for Latin men; they are less confused than American men about how sensitive they should be and whether to open doors, and are just men, which makes it easier to just be a woman around them. He gallantly asks if he can take the empty seat next to mine at the movie, and we whisper a few remarks about films we've seen lately before the lights go down. He helps me off with my jacket, and his sure, gentlemanly touch makes popcorn explode under my skin. In the dark, I can barely watch the movie because two hundred pounds of male pheromones are sitting right next to me, transmitting wildly, uniquely attuned to mine. I want to lean in to smell him better, rub my face right into his soft sweater. Every time he shifts his hand on the armrest I jump; I feel like I'm fifteen and on my first date at the movies, practically trembling at his proximity.

Doug invites us to an after-party at the corner bar. Gustavo and I sit in a red leather booth and drink too much champagne and then beer when the champagne runs out. We talk about Japanese novels and Italian films until long after Doug leaves and they start putting chairs up on the tables. Born in Brazil, Gustavo has been speaking English for only ten years but has read all the literature I hold dear; he likes the same books and films and is absolutely certain about his tastes. He treats me like a woman, but a smart woman, which is one of those feats foreign men are good at without ever feeling threatened or, God forbid, emasculated. I've known Gustavo for a few hours and I feel like I've always known him, or maybe always wanted to know him.

We kiss in the cab on the way back to the Village, where I am staying. There's nothing better than being tipsy and kissing a hunky Brazilian man in the back of a New York City cab. When I get out, he holds the door for me, and I tell him how much fun I had and that if it weren't three o'clock in the morning, I'd invite him up for a drink.

"What's so special about three o'clock in the morning?" he asks, in that soft accent, with a sly smile, and it is impossible to argue; I can't come up with any smart response whatsoever.

For the next few days, we barely leave the apartment, surfacing only for beer and cupcakes before diving back under the covers. I don't usually prefer a certain physical type in men; I'm democratic, and if you lined up all the guys I've dated, you wouldn't find much in common beyond XY genes and an edgy sense of humor. But in Gustavo I recognize my animal ideal. He might not turn heads at a bar, but he's medium-tall and strong, soft around the edges from loving good food, with thick, straight black hair, dark eyes, and a little beard stubble. He's the very image of Brenda Starr's Basil St. John—her mysterious disappearing boyfriend—without the eye patch. More than that, there's something about him that's so quietly sure of himself, so manly, in bed and out; he's one of those few men who makes me feel 100 percent female. He stops using my name and just calls me "Sexy." He slays me, over and over.

"You're a sweetheart," I tell him, kissing his chest.

He shakes his head. "You're the sweetheart," he says. "I'm just a sweetheart-in-training."

We finally venture out of the apartment and walk to a theatre to see a tragic Vittorio De Sica film, and at the end, peeking behind the sleeve covering my face, he wipes a tear off my cheek with his thumb. On the way home, he holds my hand, fingers interlaced, and walks curbside, as if protecting me from the splashes of passing cabs. I'm leaving, and he has a new gig; I sense that our own little film is coming to an end. But it's early summer, it's New York, and for those few blocks I have the world's sweetest, sexiest Brazilian boyfriend.

Home from the East Coast, I take a walk one day with my friend Cecilia. As we climb up one of San Francisco's Twin Peaks, to a sweeping view of the city from bridge to bridge, I mention that I need to come up with something worthwhile to do, something that will get me out of my head and out into the world. My brain keeps flitting back to Gustavo—who, after a flurry of e-mails, seems to be out of sight, out of mind—and to the general problem of being single in my forties; I'm having trouble creating positive, forward momentum in the rest of my life. But seeing all those accomplished classmates at the reunion who had made real contributions and being in a liberal arts atmosphere reminded me of the responsibilities that go along with the privilege of a good education—with being alive, really—and lit a fire under me.

I tell Cecilia I am tired of writing peppy articles that fill the space between ads in women's magazines, boosting women's self-confidence on one page so it can be torn down on the next. I want to do something useful, worthwhile.

Cecilia walks along quietly for a while, and then something

pops into her mind. She says her friend Carmen, a social worker in Rome, has a new job, working with a program that rescues immigrant women who have been sex-trafficked in Italy, promised a job in a pizzeria and ending up a prostitute, enslaved. Italy, alone in Europe, offers these women not only a chance to escape but help to stay in the country.

"It's a good story, no?" Cecilia asks.

Sì. The prospect of a real story, in Italy, no less—which I am able to sell to an international women's magazine—makes me forget entirely about the urgent problem of needing a new life. It also stops my obsessive wondering about whether Gustavo will ever call or whether I'll see him again. We exchanged a few e-mails, his addressed to Sexy, mine using up all the Brazilian endearments I knew, and then the correspondence fizzled out. For all my fantasies, maybe it had just been a fling—a wildly fun fling, and not everything has to last forever, but still. A friend remarked that maybe the problem was that *I* was the one who needed to be the hot Brazilian in a relationship, so to speak. "You're the exotic and creative one; your guy needs to be a little more stable," she said. "Otherwise, it's just one zany adventure after the next." In any case, once again, I decide to fly away.

I arrive in Rome and visit Carmen, the social worker, who is in her fifties and divorced. Every evening, Carmen takes me along to a different dinner party, because her circle of friends can't stand the thought of her trying to microwave something to eat at home alone (she's the only Italian I know, male or female, whose cooking is truly atrocious). Italian women are never really alone, because Italians, bless them, tend to crowd around their unattached friends until they safely find someone. Carmen has a houseful of people—an African daughter she adopted, a boarder, and now a guest from the United States—but that doesn't prevent her friends from considering her in mandatory need of company. There is no direct translation of "loneliness" in Italian—or, for that matter, "privacy." The concepts don't quite exist in Italy.

Not that Italian women don't have their own problems with men and relationships. Even more than Americans, they're caught between expectations of being good, traditional Italian girls and wives, looking after men who have never washed a dish or made a bed, and being sophisticated professionals; the dilemma leaves a lot of them unmarried, without children, and the Italian birthrate is the lowest in the world. Somehow, though, they don't seem to have the hardness that a lot of American women have, and even 1970s feminists like Carmen have no Puritan-inspired problems reconciling their ideology with dressing glamorously and provocatively. Italian women in their fifties and sixties just seem to be all that much sexier for how well they know themselves and how assured they are about their charms.

During the day, when Carmen is working, these friends invite me to lunch, one by one, as if they'd worked out a schedule. I'm never alone for a meal. Somehow, in Italy, you always feel held—if not by a man, then by a family of friends.

WHEN I ARRIVE at the Naples train station, I remember that this is where I said good-bye to the Professor after we first met on the island of Ischia and spent four sun-drenched days there, a sweet reward for getting up out of my postdivorce depression and traveling by myself. At the time, I was sure I would never see him again but felt delighted to have been able to run into him, to have spent those wonderful days in his company—eating fresh pasta, making love, swimming in the sea, and starting all over again. Now it's been four years, and I know this time that if I do see him again, it won't be as a lover. But that's fine, too. I'm moving ahead and haven't lost those years I spent with him. All those beautiful moments—sipping wine and staring at the volcanoes in the distance, making love with open eyes, wandering around Moroccan alleys holding hands—don't go away. The love in your life adds up.

I step out of the train station into soft light that shows off Naples' faded Renaissance beauty at her best. Naples is sometimes called the northernmost city in Africa for its sultry air, chaotic humanity, and medinalike mazes of ancient streets. To be in Naples again is an unexpected pleasure, because the city is irresistible in its charms: perfect pizzas, splendid decay, crumbling treasures, and evening parades of tanned and meticulously turned out couples. The volcanic islands in the distance are silhouetted against the darkly shimmering sea. I have an appointment in front of the Museo Archeologico Nazionale in a couple hours—enough time to wander the waterfront, explore the little streets and stores in Spaccanapoli, and marvel at the treasures of Pompeii in the museum.

I've never spent time in Naples by myself. This is the first time since my divorce that I've been to Italy without the Professor. Only a couple hours by train from Rome, where there are single women everywhere, like in any major industrialized city in the world, southern Italy looks upon single women suspiciously, with pity sometimes, and a whiff of disrepute. A woman dining alone in a southern Italian restaurant, relishing her food and wine, might be completely content with herself and her spaghetti alle scoglie but treated like prey by the waiter and as contagious by the Sunday-dinner guests. In southern Italy, women don't often go out by themselves, at least not in the evening or to partake of a meal; their husbands, family members, or female friends almost always accompany them in public. This is true, to a lesser extent, of the men, too; Italians don't like to do anything alone.

STANDING BY MYSELF in the wide stone piazza in front of the Museo Archeologico Nazionale, waiting for Giusi, a social worker who is going to help me do research, I feel nervous—a target. Naples, of course, has a dangerous reputation, with its mafioso underbelly, its petty and not-so-petty thievery, anarchic traffic, and casual attitude toward history and human life. But it's no more dangerous, really, than New York or any other big American city; you just have to act smart, tuck away your jewelry, and look as if you know where you're going.

A tough-looking boy, a hoodlum, maybe ten years old, approaches me, and I hold my passport and money tighter to my body. I glare at him, and he crosses his arms and opens his legs in a wider stance, like an annoyed Italian grown-up man, then calls my name. He's here to meet me instead of his mother. Carlino takes my arm, a perfect little gentleman, steps off the sidewalk, and brazenly stops traffic with an authoritative hand signal, only the drivers' hands moving in a vast repertoire of gestures of impatience. It's sweet to be back in Italy, where even little boys look out for you if you're a woman—not belittlingly, but protectively, in a courteous way.

Carlino leads me to a tall, narrow stone building, laundry hanging on the balcony above. Inside, I meet Giusi, a single mom who works to rescue sex-trafficked women. She seems frazzled but kisses me enthusiastically and makes me an espresso. We'll need the coffee, because we'll be up most of the night, scouting for immigrant women who are enslaved and forced to work as prostitutes. A neighbor drops by to stay with Carlino, who is watching soccer on TV, screaming and punching the air every few minutes when someone makes a play. He jumps to his feet, unprompted, when we leave, and shakes my hand.

Giusi and I meet up with two coworkers. Though their task for the evening is serious, they are Italians and hospitable, and so they first take me to a famous pizzeria, L'Antica Pizzeria Da Michele, before we set out at night. There is a huge crowd outside the pizzeria, and it seems like it will take all night to get a table. But somehow, with the right word to someone, the long line melts like mozzarella and we are sitting down. This is the oldest and best pizzeria in Naples and so the world. It's a small place for all its glory, and its offerings are few, but the wood-fired pizza—with spicy extra-virgin olive oil and fior di latte cheese puddling among the fresh herbs and tomatoes—is enough reason itself to go to Naples.

Soon we've paid the check, maneuvered a van out of an impossible parking spot, and then, abruptly, we're in an entirely different atmosphere, cruising the roads near the train station. I'm not prepared to suddenly shift from the beautiful, dreamlike Italy to such a harsh, dirty reality. I wake up and realize I'm here to work. Suddenly, all the beauty of Italy has been swept aside like a curtain, revealing a dark and seamy underside, a side I've never seen, where young girls stand on the curbs, shivering, waiting for a strange man in a car to pull up and let them in.

The social workers spend each night offering the women working the streets a little warmth, some coffee, medical advice, condoms, and a ready ear to listen to their problems. When we slow down to approach the girls, most wave us away fearfully. We pass groups of girls from Nigeria, Ukraine, Albania. Most of the girls, Giusi tells me, thought they were coming to Italy to make money working in a hair salon or a bar or as an au pair. Maybe some suspected, but they felt they had no choice but to leave the poverty they were living in; nothing, they believed, could be worse. Most grasped it as an opportunity, a way out. "They were doing the best they could, taking the only chance they had, to help themselves and their families," she tells me.

None of the women anticipated or could have imagined, in their darkest moments, what would actually happen: the people who had made those promises smuggled them into Italy; took away their passports; beat, raped, and brutalized them; and kept them imprisoned except for the hours when they were forced to work the streets, spilling their purses at the end of the day and keeping all the money to repay an ever-mounting debt.

The immigrants, most of whom barely speak Italian, usually

work twelve-hour shifts, engaging in quick sexual encounters in clients' cars or behind bushes by the road. Their pimps monitor their every move by cell phone, so even grabbing a coffee in a passing van is dangerous for them.

At one desolate corner, we stop and let a Nigerian, Marika, into the van. She's working alone, and Giusi reminds her, as she makes an espresso on the van's little stove, that it's a lot safer to work with someone else. Marika shrugs helplessly. Up close she looks so young and vulnerable. She's wearing a miniskirt that barely covers her bottom, gold eye shadow, a ratty pair of high-heeled black boots, long fake black braids, and a top that reveals false breasts. (Giusi explains to me later that the girls often wear plastic breasts, not to appear sexier but to protect what little they can protect of themselves and their feelings, to keep the men from touching their real breasts.)

Marika warms her hands and waits for the espresso to brew. She complains that there isn't much work this evening, because there are too many police in the area. Prostitution on the streets is legal in Italy, but the girls get hassled anyway. She sips her coffee slowly, to make it last, and says she's worried because she still owes $15,000 to the people who brought her here, even though she's already paid them $40,000—at about $5 per five-minute trick. She has a calculator always running in her head.

I ask her how long she has until she's free. She looks at me suspiciously, and I slide my notebook out of view.

"Who the fuck is she?" she asks, quickly turning to Giusi, her tough question hiding her terror. "Is she the police or something?"

"No, no," says Giusi, patting her arm. "She helps us. She's a nurse. She brings us condoms."

I smile and rip open a condom, then blow it up to a huge size. "Best kind," I say.

Marika laughs at the balloon like a child. I bat it into the air toward her, and it falls to the floor. Her smile fades. "Two more years," she tells me wearily, "and I can do some other kind of work." It may be longer, though, if her recent luck holds up—not long ago she was robbed at gunpoint, she tells me, by a client who took all her money.

"When I came here," she says, "I thought I was getting a job at a supermarket." She rolls her eyes at her childish naiveté—she was nineteen then, and now she's a much older, harder twenty-one. But at least, she tells me, she doesn't have the problems the Albanian women on the street have. "The Albanian women are raped by their pimps, but not the Africans," she tells me in her broken Italian. "The Albanians hit them. All I have to do is pay back my debt."

I am shocked by her story. I want to whisk her away, take her back to my hotel, run a hot shower, hand her a fluffy towel, find her some new clothes, drive her to the train station, and buy her a ticket away from here. But she is being watched.

Giusi tells Marika that she knows some girls who never paid back all of their debt, and they're working somewhere else now, not on the streets. Nothing bad ever happened to them. This is the real reason behind the roaming van, to help these girls escape.

Marika considers that, then dismisses it. "No," she says, "they lie all the time."

"Really, it's true," says Giusi, but she can't push. If the organized criminals who traffic in women found out she was encouraging the prostitutes to escape, the van would become a target. As it is, it's only barely tolerated by the police and racketeers. All Giusi can do is hint and hope that Marika finds the widely distributed pamphlets and the courage to call the *numero verde,* the free "green" number to get help.

Maybe someday Marika will make that call, but not tonight. Tonight she's too scared. She doesn't trust Giusi when she says there's a way out. Marika got into her present situation by trusting someone who was going to "help" her out of poverty by bringing her to Italy. She doesn't trust the fact that I'm in the van, since she's never seen me before. She can't afford to trust anyone.

Marika's cell phone rings, and she jumps. She drops her plastic coffee cup and, without saying good-bye, slips back out into the night.

ALL OF THE girls I talk to—in the van, in Trieste, and in a safe house in Rome—left home out of desperation, but also out of some sense of gumption. They craved adventure and independence; they wanted to see something of the world, to be someone. A crack opened in their world, one where they had almost no choices or independence, and they slipped out, having no idea that their kidnappers were ready to pounce, exploiting that smallest urge for freedom, for which they'd pay an unspeakable price.

Kira, a Nigerian hairdresser I met at the safe house, was offered work in Italy at a shoe factory. Kidnapped, forced to hike over the mountains to the sea, then crossing in a dinghy, she ended up in Italy with a $40,000 debt; when she escaped and contacted her family, she found out that the thugs had beaten her mother in Nigeria so badly she would never again walk without limping. Serious, intelligent Dara, a dark-haired, twenty-one-year-old Moldavian computer programmer, was abducted, raped, and sold. A friend of her boyfriend had told her he could find her work in Italy in a pizzeria, and before she could think it through or say good-bye to her family, a group of men with cell phones took her and several other girls to Hungary, changing cars several times along the way. They were taken to a house where men came to look them over, touching their bodies and genitals, and when they left with the men they understood that they had been sold. She was forced to work on the streets in Bologna and to have anal sex with clients to double her price. When she tried to escape, her boss beat her viciously, locked her in a bathroom without food, then sold her again, to a group of Albanians. After working for several more months, always accompanied by men who held her head down in the car on the way to work, a client helped her escape.

AT AN INNOCUOUS house in the suburbs of Rome a week before, I watched Dara, cheerfully clearing the table as the other girls did the dishes, taking turns holding a baby, and wondered how she could be so resilient. But watching more closely, I could see that the girls did only what the social workers told them, no more. Whatever gumption they'd had was gone. Anna, a psychologist who works with the girls, told me it's hard for the girls to take an active role in shaping their own lives, since they did what other people told them to do in order to survive, turning themselves into machines, repressing their thoughts of autonomy, relying on their captors. Many of them are passive, thinking that what happened to them happened because they're fundamentally weak. Others feel punished for having left their families, for having stepped out of line. They focus on making money, as if their debt still exists. Some of them constantly wash their hands, obsessively, as a way of trying to rid themselves of their dirty experience. But the very fact that they lived through the experience and managed to escape, Anna said, is a basis, though shaky, for rebuilding their self-esteem. "These girls have survived," she said. "Now they have to take their lives into their own hands."

It's the girls who played a more active role in their stories, the ones who took off for reasons of opportunity or even adventure, who have the best chance of recovering a sense of self, Anna told me. They don't see themselves entirely as victims and are more apt to be able to work their way out of the degradation, humiliation, and violence they experienced. In some ways, finally, after all they've been through, the terrible price they've paid, they may realize that they've managed to make their dream of living and working in Italy come true. Now they can start afresh and get a job in a boutique or trattoria. The challenge will be whether they can rewrite their stories, no longer be victimized or passive but able to heal themselves and somehow become the agents of their own lives. Giusi and my friend Carmen are doing all they can—single women devoting themselves to helping out other single, unprotected women—but at some point the girls will have to take over. I am amazed at the strength that has taken the girls this far, engineering their escapes and starting over, even if they are still in shock.

I know that for weeks after, my heart will be breaking for these girls. The consequences of their efforts to be independent are so much harsher than for American women; there's no comparison. In their native countries, they too have grown up in a new world that requires them to work, both in the home and outside, but they're severely limited in their movements, punished if they do what they must to survive. They're protected as long as they adhere strictly to traditions, in cultures whose global demands no longer make that possible. They crave the freedom, education, and experiences that go along with the new roles they've taken on—they want to travel, have boyfriends, buy pink hoodies and silver tennis shoes—but they're at risk of rape, exploitation, and slavery. They're caught between the old and new worlds, bearing the brunt of the ambivalence and anger about how women and the world are changing.

LATE AT NIGHT, after we've made the rounds in the van, Giusi and the other social workers drop me off at my hotel. She offers to pick me up in the morning to accompany me to the train station, but I tell her I'm fine, I can take care of myself. I appreciate that it's a natural part of the culture to take care of single women, but I don't feel vulnerable. I can call a taxi.

I think about how easy it is for me to travel alone, how much real independence I enjoy. I can't get the images of Marika and the other girls out of my head. It's such a luxury to travel when women all over the world are constantly coming up against constraints to their freedoms, testing the limits out of desire or need, almost always paying a price that is measured by their culture: sometimes loneliness and uncertainty; financial instability; sometimes fear for their safety, their lives; sometimes the horrible brutality and violence the immigrant women I've met on this trip have endured. There is an uneasy balance everywhere of cultures wanting to protect and control women, allowing them some autonomy out of economic necessity, then punishing them for taking it, leaving them without any protection at all.

Italy has probably managed a better balance than most, making it possible for women to feel independent yet protected and included even if they aren't married and don't have their own children. Single women in Italy are always part of a larger family, whether bound by blood or by friendship.

Leaving Naples after three weeks of talking with Italian social workers, sex-trafficked women, and prostitutes' advocates, I feel glad to be able at least to write something about them. That's such a small thing to do. It seems like an obligation to use the advantages of my independence to bring to light stories of other women who are suffering for their small attempts at freedom. (I write the story and turn it in, but six months later, the magazine changes top editors; the new editor kills the piece, saying, "We've just had too many sex slave stories lately," as if she were talking about fashion spreads featuring hobo bags. Eventually I give it to an online publication, where it's up for a day, and then present it to an audience at a global grassroots women's organization event where, at least, the participants care.)

Every time I encounter women who have survived such dire circumstances, with unacknowledged bravery and resilience, I'm overcome with gratitude for my freedom and a desire to do more. Whatever price I feel I have paid for independence in my life is insignificant compared with theirs.

I buy my train ticket, find my seat in the compartment, nod to the other passengers, and head back to Rome.

Chapter Five

UPOLU AND SAVAI'I,
WESTERN SAMOA

2002

The Samoan islands, floating in the South Pacific at the edge of the international date line, look like Hawaii in a time warp. There are the same rugged mountains, lush rain forests, and wide sandy beaches but no high-rise hotels or honeymooners in sight. The jungle at the perimeter of the runway is thick, startlingly green, and threatening to take over the tarmac by tomorrow. The air is thick and sweet as mango flesh, so warm that if Samoans could, they would probably dress only in their tattoos. Instead, everyone wears light T-shirts and sea-colored sarongs called lavalavas.

I'm here doing a story about gender blurring in Samoa— really, about a third gender, called *fa'afafine*. I've hardly been home these months, which suits me down to the ground, though I'm vaguely plotting to get back to New York to see Gustavo. That's foolish, I know; by this time I should be able to see through the fog of romance and hope and realize that if it had been anything more than a fling, I would've heard from him. I am always working myself up into frenzies about men and finding myself disappointed that things don't turn out happily ever after, but then I don't see why I should have to exclude myself from that falling-in-love fantasy. I know that expectations can poison beautiful moments and too easily transform them into resentments, but I keep hoping one of these flings will last. It's hard to say whether such a delicious encounter thousands of miles from home is worth the feeling of longing later on. As a traveler, I know it's impossible to repeat amazing chance experiences, you have to appreciate them fully for the moment you're there; life is just a series of those present moments, adding up. But as a woman, I want to be back in his arms, or in the arms of someone I know will still be there tomorrow, who'll take care of me. I realize I'm always falling for men far from home, then flying away. Still.

So here I am, on the way to the South Pacific. I got this Samoa assignment because I recently wrote an article about a friend who switched genders—the article was unfortunately and sensationally headlined "My Ex-boyfriend Became a Woman"—so the editors figured I must be an expert on the topic.

I'm not, but my friend is. She is still basically the same person, different pronoun—except with highlights and happier with herself. She hasn't lost her sense of humor: when she pulls out the hormone pills she's taking, she says, "This one makes you cry at movies and want to be in a relationship, and this one makes you hate professional wrestling and the Three Stooges." She has a new softness about her that is more than physical. Talking about it, she says she also has an unexpected new sense of vulnerability that came along with her new vagina. I am amazed that after forty-two years of being male she feels that physical sense of vulnerability so strongly—maybe because it's so new—but that fear of violation is, for women, built into the anatomy.

We were roommates in New York City for a while, twenty years ago; at the time he always liked me, he said, because I was "a feminist who could still wear pink socks." We started a little romance that fizzled out after an awkward sexual encounter. For years I thought it was my fault—I was young and inexperienced and worried I wasn't sexy enough or doing things right. Finding out that he was a she, all those years later, was, selfishly, a relief—and a Note to Self that when things don't work out with a man, you can't always blame yourself. So that was all good. Going shopping with her, on the other hand, was annoying as hell, since everything fit her perfectly—she's a biological *male* after all—while everything was too tight on my curves, proving that designers have a warped and probably misogynistic sense of the female form.

In any case, after a year, I almost forget that she was ever a he. When the editor calls with the Samoa assignment, I can hardly claim to be an expert in the topic of the social-versus-biological construction of gender, but having dug around in that territory, I am fascinated. I even have a third cousin who is married to a Samoan, so I have a place to start—though being fundamentalist Christians, my cousins are a little confused when I call them asking if they know any Samoan drag queens. But they're helpful, and I'm as excited as the young Margaret Mead to be heading off to Samoa.

*   *   *

AT THE AIRPORT in Upolu, I glance around, and, in their similar
dress, it's hard to tell Samoan men and women apart—especially
since the women have big biceps encircled with tattoo armbands
and the men have luxurious long black hair and gold-hooped ears.
Samoans of both genders are big-boned, hearty types, evolved
from people who were strong enough to paddle from island to
island to survive, who were quick enough to escape rival tribes,
and who fed on the starchy breadfruit and taro roots that grow
everywhere on the islands. They're like tropical flowers—big,
bright, and meaty, with a humid, amorphous sexuality.

I find a battered lime green taxi, shell necklaces dangling
from the rearview mirror, greet the driver—*"Talofa!"*—and set
off with a squeal. We whiz by thatched huts on stilts near the
beach, nut brown children laughing and playing in bright blue
waves. The villages are tidy, with a profusion of bougainvillea,
red ginger, pink hibiscus, and exotic flowers I've never seen. The
place exudes relaxation, as if the vibrant colors are soaking up all
the available intensity.

We arrive in Apia, where modern offices stand next to palm-
thatched houses, rickety food stands, and open-air markets. Near
the center of town, across the street from the harbor, we pull up
at Aggie Grey's, an incongruously stately, rambling, white colonial hotel with bellhops in red uniforms out front. This place,
the oldest hotel in town, was built decades ago, when adventur-
ers wanted a civilized respite between their forays into the savage wilds and World War II GIs needed a real hamburger for

a change. After the war, it became a chic getaway for the Hollywood set, farther even than Tahiti, where stars like Gary Cooper, William Holden, and Marlon Brando could sit by the pool and know that no one could possibly know who they were, except that they were rich.

I've arranged lunch with a famous Samoan fa'afafine. An anthropologist gave me her name, along with some background about the fa'afafine, which means "in the way of a woman." Men who openly dress as women are an accepted part of life in Samoa, are treated as women, and play the same roles in Samoan culture as genetic women: caretakers, teachers, Bible school leaders. They're also entertainers, able to get away with doing some of the things women used to do in Samoa that have been frowned on since Christian missionaries came around 1830, such as dancing provocatively for visiting guests. Samoans are a little huffy when talking about sex and gender, saying that people have been making a lot of assumptions about Samoa ever since the young and gullible Margaret Mead solemnly recorded every joking story told to her about the supposed promiscuity on the islands in 1928. Today fa'afafine are treated like ladies—except that men are more likely to banter and make bawdy jokes with them.

At the hotel, Sonia is sitting by the pool, under an umbrella, wearing a tight flowered tank top, miniskirt, and heels. She has beautiful dancer's legs and an erect posture. Only the extra layer of makeup shows her sixtyish age, and nothing reveals her biology.

I greet her, and she kisses me and gestures to the stage. "I used to dance here, from the time I was nine." She gazes at the stage, the canopy of painted bark cloth, the pots of tropical flowers and ferns. "I was the star of the show. I was the best."

"I'm sure you still are," I say, and Sonia waves away those bygone years with her long coral nails. A waiter comes by with drinks. He says, "Excuse me," to Sonia, and they both snicker. After he leaves, she explains that the way he said "Excuse me" doubles in Samoan for "Suck me." Fa'afafine are famous for their sexual double entendres and teasing, she says, and waiters know they can get away with it. I make a note never to say "excuse me" in Samoa.

We sip our mai tais as Sonia relates her history. There were always "aunties" in her family. Her father was a high chief in the village—a *matai*—and from a young age, she liked to play the role of the princess, serving drinks in the kava ceremony. She loved to dance, hopping up on stage as early as three to perform for the village families, twirling around in a little skirt as people laughed when they could see what was underneath. "Deep inside, I've always known myself to be a woman."

Sonia started having sex with other boys when she was nine or ten. Back in those days—contrary to what Margaret Mead wrote—most girls wouldn't have sex with boys before marriage. Fa'afafine were another story. "We filled in the gaps," Sonia says. These days, of course, more girls sleep with men before marriage—especially the young tourist *palagi*s from Australia, New Zealand, and the United States—but boys still "practice" with fa'afafine. That doesn't make them gay or bisexual, Sonia explains, because fa'afafine are considered women. "Gay men are only interested in sleeping with other gay men, they're fully male." A fa'afafine would never sleep with another fa'afafine, because it would be considered lesbian and therefore taboo.

I try to keep track of all this and scan the restaurant, considering that many of the men here, as well as the macho, muscular, tattooed men I saw walking around Apia earlier, have had sex with other men, with fa'afafine, and considered it straight sex. The women are still pressured by the church to wait until marriage. All in all, it's a pretty good deal for the men.

Sonia sips her drink and glances back to the stage. "Marlon Brando!" She lifts up her feet and points her polished toes. "Marlon loved to watch me dance." She leans toward me. "He didn't know . . . well . . . let's say he was surprised." She laughs, throwing her head back and shaking her long, dark hair.

SONIA GIVES ME names of other fa'afafine, and for the next two days, I track them down—dancing at a club, playing netball, watching a thrilling rugby game against Tonga. In just a few days, people begin to wave to me on the street. I go a little native, learning to tie a sarong and wearing it with a T-shirt, as everyone does on the street—though when I show up that way at a club, a young fa'afafine scolds me, telling me to go home and dress up, girl, no one dresses like that to go out.

When I return to the palm-thatched club wearing jeans and high-heeled sandals, I sit with a friendly young woman I met at the hotel and her friends. Soon the lights dim and drumming starts. A troupe of dancers enters the stage—the men in aqua lavalavas and black tattoos that circle their waists like giant bat wings or cover their legs like bicycle shorts, the fa'afafine in coconut bras and grass skirts. It looks as though it'll be a cheesy talent show, but from the start, everyone dances as if it's the purpose of their lives.

When the applause for the floor show stops, everyone in the audience gets up to dance. The girls pull me, and I can't help but follow them onstage, doing whatever approximation of Samoan dancing I can muster, something like flamenco on acid at a Grateful Dead show. Everyone laughs—with me, at me, it doesn't matter. They all dance, dazed by the drumming, exhilarated. Each of my body parts seems to be responding to a different rhythm. I've left my mind, my story, my culture, everything but my body back at the table with my beer, and I dance and dance.

It's delirious—to be included as an outsider, to have stumbled into such a colorful group of revelers. All that dancing feels like shedding a skin. By the time I return to my hotel, I'm exhausted with exhilaration. I jump into the pool, float, and stare at the unfamiliar stars, content. If I had a husband and children, I wouldn't be out dancing with Samoan drag queens and floating in tropical pools.

THE LAST EVENING in Apia, I meet Sonia in the bar. She's wearing a leopard-printed mini with a stretch lace black top and is accompanied by Tini, a burly fa'afafine with a flower tucked behind one ear and gopher-size biceps. The waiter flirts outrageously with them, giving Sonia a squeeze around the waist.

"Do the men still see fa'afafine after they're married?" I ask, when the waiter leaves.

"It's still cheating, but it's more cheating to be with another woman," says Sonia. "That's when the wives really get ferocious."

"Being with a fa'afafine is like a joke to the wife," says Tini, shrugging her giant shoulders.

It's not much of a joke, really: knowing you are a woman but that men won't take you seriously. Wanting to have a husband and children and not being able to manage it. I'm beginning to identify too closely with these fa'afafine, I think, and I have another drink. The fan twirls on the ceiling, and I realize we've all become quiet. "But did you ever fall in love?" I ask.

Sonia sighs. "We have women's feelings, so of course we fall in love." She waves this thought away and begins ticking off several long-term boyfriends she's had.

"But the men always eventually leave," says Tini, shaking her head. "They go with women who will give them children."

"Do you have children?" Sonia asks, ignoring Tini's last remark, and I shake my head no.

"Why not?" asks Tini. "Children are beautiful."

"Never met the right father, I guess." I twirl the parasol in my drink.

"But you're not so old, you're still attractive," says Tini. "Why don't you have a husband?"

"I don't know." They look at me expectantly. "I had a husband, but we split up, and since then . . . I guess I've been busy working."

Sonia puts her hand on her hip and shifts her legs in her mini-skirt. "You have a job like a man, traveling by yourself," she scolds me. "Maybe a man wants someone who is more like a woman."

It's making me uneasy, having a fake woman tell me I'm not acting enough like a real one.

Later, in my room—after more drinking with the fa'afafine and dancing with tattooed Samoan men—I am too rattled to sleep, though it's the middle of the night. I flip on the TV and see that the Brazilians have just won the World Cup. I know that on the other side of the world, Gustavo is going crazy, and I want to talk to him, hear his voice, feel his presence, congratulate him. I dial all the international codes, and when I get his answering machine, I hang up.

THE NEXT DAY, I leave Upolu for Savai'i, a more traditional Samoan island, to see how village fa'afafine are different from the big-city girls. From the plane, a little puddle jumper, velvety green islands rise out of the turquoise sea. Savai'i's outermost piece of land, a panhandle called the Falealupo Peninsula, floats near the international date line, edging toward yesterday. The lush peninsula is considered the entrance to the underworld, the place where the sun sets into the sea, where the spirits roam freely at night but return to their terrible caves and fires by daybreak. From the air, Savai'i seems much bigger and wilder than Upolu, matted with rain forests, its jagged ridge of volcanic craters raised like the backbone of a dark and ancient sea monster.

The plane lands on a strip cleared in a dense jungle of banyan trees, propellers winding down. A few villagers in rust-rimmed cars greet the other passengers, but there are no taxis. I hitch a ride with a school principal, who offers that he's going that way anyway. We bump our way over dirt to the main paved road that circles the island, passing open-walled houses, oval thatched huts, and cacophonous tropical gardens.

We chat, and he can't understand that I came so far to write about fa'afafine, whom Samoans hardly think twice about. "Why don't you write about how our islands are sinking into the sea instead?" asks the principal. He explains that global warming is affecting people who have no fault in creating the problem and can do nothing to change it. I agree that it would be a better story.

"When Manhattan starts to sink, the magazines will pay attention," I tell him, and he smiles broadly.

He points to a group of huts with corrugated steel roofs. "This is your hotel." He gives me the name of a fa'afafine I could talk to, a schoolteacher named Tara, and draws a map of where she lives.

I wander around the resort, a main house with a wide porch upstairs and some landscaped oval *fales* set around a wide grassy yard, with clusters of ginger stalks waving their waxy red flowers. My little hut is screened, with matchstick blinds, two cots, one frayed pink towel, a cold-water shower, and a cistern of drinking water. Tall coconut palms line the road, and across the street, a white beach seems to stretch forever.

I gather my things for the beach. As long as it's Sunday, I'm taking the day off. I wander across the road and climb over a rock wall to the beach. It's the kind of beach you dream of, the kind you never find when you go on a package tour that advertises a beach just like this one: fine white sand, palm trees, no trash, no people, no nothing but beach and water as far as you can see.

I unwrap my lavalava, spread it out on the sand, slather on sunscreen, and lean against a warm rock, reading. The sun penetrates layers of my skin until I'm glowing from inside like an ember. I dash across the burning sand and plunge into the water, swimming out far around a jutting rock. Then I float, letting the gently rocking water take me where it will.

I swim back, not because I can't swim far but because there is no one on the beach to say, as the Professor always would, "Stay a little closer to shore." I have to be that person for myself, the one who doesn't trust her own strength or the gentle tides. Stay a little closer to shore.

I flop down on the sarong, then doze. I sense a presence and open my eyes. Not far down the beach, a large Samoan man is walking. I suddenly feel alone. I stand up, quickly shake the sand out of the lavalava, and wrap myself. I gather my things and start to walk along the beach, safer in motion.

The only time I was ever assaulted, the only time in all my travels I've ever been in serious danger—if you don't count visiting Baghdad ten days before the first Persian Gulf War as a guest of Saddam Hussein, with no confirmed ticket back to Jordan—was when I was alone on a beach. It was twenty years ago. I'd been traveling in Egypt with another woman, who was fifteen years older—younger than I am now, I realize. She'd seemed so old then. I met Edie on an Israeli kibbutz where I worked as a volunteer for three months—fishing, picking dates, cleaning used flypaper off of grapefruit trees—and we decided to travel on to Egypt together. We both wanted to explore the Sinai Desert, the tombs of Luxor, the ancient temples and pyramids, but from the moment we arrived in Cairo, we realized it wasn't so easy to travel around, we couldn't leave each other's side. Men constantly called out and hissed, tried to pull pieces of our hair or "accidentally" brush our breasts.

Even together, we felt threatened. We took a bus to the Red Sea, where the guidebook mentioned there were beautiful, peaceful beaches. The bus let us out in the center of a small town, with few tourists, where most of the women covered their heads with scarves. We wrapped scarves around our heads, too, so as not to attract attention or offend anyone.

After finding a little pensione, we went to the beach, a couple of miles from town, and found a nice sheltered spot near some rocks. I wanted to go for a walk, but Edie wouldn't come along; her energy level didn't match mine. I was tired of constantly being by her side; if I could just take a walk by myself for half an hour, I'd be content to be in her company again.

We were far from town, there was no one anywhere, so I walked vigorously along the beach, feeling free in shorts and a T-shirt, moving my limbs, stretching out after days and days of slow motion. Then up on the bluffs I noticed a figure in a djellabah. I kept on walking.

"How much for you?" he called out, and I ignored him.

"How much for you? One pound? Two pounds?" I walked faster, until I could no longer see him on the bluff.

I turned a corner, around a hill that tumbled into the sea, and there he was, down on the beach, coming toward me. "How much for you?" he asked, his mouth open and wetly pink under his thick mustache.

"*Em-shee bayeed,*" I replied, the only Arabic phrase I knew: get lost. He snickered.

"My husband is over there," I said, pointing, turning to walk back.

"No husband," he said, coming closer.

"Yes," I said, and he grabbed my arm. "No!" I screamed and knew no one could hear.

As he began roughing my breasts, a calmness and clarity washed over me. A movie I'd seen, maybe one of those high school gym class movies about self-defense, started playing in my mind. I followed it, as in a trance. I went limp and could feel him relax his grip in response. Then I gathered up all my strength at once, an energy bolt through my body, and shoved the palm of my hand straight up his nose. He reeled back, surprised. I stepped forward and, with all my sturdy-legged force, shoved a knee into his groin. He fell down, doubling over in the sand, and I had an instant to make a decision.

I've always been strong but slow, good on endurance but not speed. If I ran, this lithe Egyptian would get up, follow, catch me, and that would be that. He could kill me. I looked at the waves. If I swam, I might make it. I *would* make it. I ran to the ocean, dived in, slipped off my shoes, untangled my shirt over my head, and swam for my life.

I swam and swam, my heart pounding in my ears, pulling

with all my strength, until I dared to turn around and see if he was swimming after me, trying to catch my toes. But he was way back on the shore, back on his feet, and I could barely make out his yelling: "How much for you?"

I swam all the way back, around the outcropping, past the bluff where I had first seen the man, until finally in the far distance I could spot Edie, sunning herself. I was relieved that she was all right and angry at myself for leaving her side. When I finally stumbled out of the water, collapsing on the sand, I let go, sobbing. Edie gave me water and a reassuring arm. She screamed about the men in that country, pigs who treat women like sheep. I said I might wish the guy were dead, but it was a different culture, not a culture I'd want to live in, but I was walking alone on their sand in an outfit that had a different meaning for them, and I should've known. I was stupid.

We walked back to town, my bare feet bleeding by the time we arrived at the hotel. I showered, changed, and took the next bus back to Cairo, where I immediately cashed my dwindling traveler's checks and booked a flight to a country I'd never visited, where I didn't speak the language, but where I knew I'd feel more at home: Italy.

That experience should have made me wary. Sure, I hadn't walked alone on the beach in a Muslim country since. But actually, it gave me an outsized sense of my strength, my ability to protect myself in a pinch. I had fought off a rapist and escaped. I still walk around streets alone, in Naples or the Tenderloin, thinking I have a secret weapon, a bolt of energy, the ability to escape from trouble and just swim away.

I hear the Samoan man on the beach call out, and flinch. I glance at the water, but Samoans are strong swimmers, so I whirl back toward the hotel. He calls, I don't know what he's saying, and then I see a little girl run out of the bushes and catch up to him. The man scoops her up, puts her on his shoulders, and continues walking. They pass me. "*Talofa,*" I say softly, eyes looking down.

"*Talofa,*" he replies, and his little daughter waves with a big, bright smile.

IN THE MORNING, in the moist heat, I throw on a lavalava and make my way over to the big house for breakfast, sitting at a table on a wooden porch with a view of the sea. I'm amazed that the waiter, Rinaldo, brings me a good cappuccino and that he's half Italian. Here, out on a remote Samoan island, I've found Italian coffee to drink with a view of the most beautiful beach, waves breaking on the coral reef a quarter mile out.

After breakfast, Rinaldo brings out a map of the island and shows me some places to go. I take off in the old Toyota I've rented, my ultimate destination the village where the principal said Tara, the fa'afafine, lives. I circle the island, stopping where Rinaldo suggested—caves, a canopy walk over a forest of ferns and banyan trees, blowholes spraying in the lava rock. I follow the map to the village of Safolava and find Tara's parents' open-air house, where pigs graze in the front yard. Inside, her mother weaves straw mats on the floor. No one speaks any English; when I say the name "Tara," her niece starts giggling. "Auntie," she says.

Tara wanders in, wearing a lavalava and a white shirt that any man might wear. Gentle and intelligent, she has short hair and a quiet femininity. She asks if we can meet tomorrow, if I could come talk to her students in English; then we can go out with another fa'afafine, a friend who lives on a plantation.

On the way back, I make one last stop at the Satuita Falls. I climb the narrow, steep trail, picking my way over rocks, until I hear and then see breathtaking jungle falls, Tarzan falls, a hypnotic gush of water crashing down from the high rain forest into a peaceful pool carved deep into the rock. The water is so clear light blue it's possible to see all the way to the bottom, and the bottom is a long way down. I dive in for a swim, dry myself with my sarong, and think that so far this has been one of the best days ever, this is why I love to travel.

THE NEXT DAY I put on a dress, pack my beach things, and drive to Tara's school. About thirty kids are out on recess in the sunny school-yard garden, exuberant with candy-striped plumeria, white ginger, and catwhisker flowers. Shy at first, the braver boys ask me to take their pictures; then they all surround me, smiling and waving. Tara walks across the yard, and the children come to order. "Thanks for coming," she says, looking me up and down. "I love your dress."

In the open-air classroom, Tara introduces me as a friend visiting from America and tells the children to ask me questions in English. They raise their hands and, as best they can, ask where I'm from, if I have brothers and sisters, and how I like Samoa.

Tara points to the map of the world to show them where San Francisco is, and they can't imagine anything that far away; most of them have never been off the island. I talk about buildings as high as a waterfall and subways that run in tunnels underground and a tall golden bridge that serves as a big gate to the bay that surrounds the city. The kids ask where my husband and children are and are more confused when I say I don't have any than they are about the subways and bridges.

"Auntie," one little boy says, and the boy next to him giggles. The word spreads through the room, and all the kids are covering their mouths to hide their laughter.

AFTER SCHOOL, TARA and I pull over to a shaded spot under some coconut trees. From a trail deep in the jungle emerges a thin, weathered fa'afafine with ratty bleached hair and a ragged tank top that shows her hard biceps. Tara introduces Lucy, who squats by the side of the road and rolls a cigarette. Tara explains that I'm writing about fa'afafine, and Lucy brags about all the beauty pageants she won years ago. She is almost as famous as Sonia, she says. "I have a lot of shiny dresses." She takes a drag on her cigarette and smooths her hair.

Tara and Lucy talk about how difficult it is to be a fa'afafine on the island—no place to go, nowhere to dress up. Lucy disappears to her hut and comes back with a pineapple she cuts with a knife, the sweetest pineapple I've ever tasted. I ask how old they were when they knew they were fa'afafine.

"I changed my life when I was seven," says Tara. "We used

to go to Sunday school, and we had to weed the plantation for the pastor, we were out in the weeds with the boys." She looks out across the field. "I still remember the boy that did it to me, he was older than me. After that boy did it to me, then other boys would do it to me in the weeds." She laughs, and I wonder how she can laugh.

Lucy wipes her mouth on her shirt. "I changed my life when I was ten. It was my brother-in-law," she says. "When my father would beat me at home because I wanted to wear dresses and dance, I would run away to my sister's house. She had a husband, maybe eighteen or nineteen, and when we went out to feed the pigs one night, he did it to me there. He showed me what was in his pants, and I didn't know what to do, and he grabbed me and pulled me down." She takes a bite of her pineapple.

"Were you scared?" I ask.

"No, I didn't tell anyone," says Lucy. "I could never speak of it to my sister, and my father would have beat me. I didn't know I was a fa'afafine then, but my brother-in-law kept doing it to me in the fields, and then other older boys would do it to me, too."

Lucy and Tara finish the pineapple, but I've lost my appetite.

"Let's go to the surfer bar," Lucy says, eyeing the car.

THE MAGOGO BEACH club is the center of the local surfer scene, with huts on the beach to rent, camping supplies for sale, and a bar. Young Australian and New Zealander surfers, tanned and tattooed, pound down the beers after a long day riding the waves.

Tara and Lucy find a table, and the waitress, a trendy-looking Samoan woman in her forties, takes their order for beers. "Big ones," says Lucy.

The first Vailimas are served, and before the waitress leaves the table, Lucy orders another round. She and Tara drink as if they don't know when in life they'll find another palagi to foot the bill, and I lose track of the rounds. The drunker they get, the less English they speak. I drink because I'm getting bored, tinged with sadness at these two fa'afafine and their gaiety, which now seems so forced.

At a nearby table, the young palagi surfers, blond and buff, are becoming raucous. "Hey," Lucy yells over in their direction. "Why don't you guys come on over and buy us a drink?" One of the young men glances over in our direction, nudges a buddy, and they all laugh uproariously.

Undeterred, Lucy swings her way over to their table and sits down. The young men seem greatly amused by her presence, and she acts as if she is wildly entertaining, not the butt of their jokes. "Come sit on my lap, baby," one says in his thick Australian accent, and the others double over laughing. Lucy slides onto his lap, and he makes obscene pumping motions, holding her waist. He pinches her breast, hard. "Are these real?" he asks, and while the others laugh at her, Lucy beams like a child.

"You're cute," she says, throwing her arms around his neck. The joke has gone too far, and he pushes her, roughly, off his lap. In her inebriated state, Lucy falls off the edge of the bench. She picks herself up, dusting sand off, stunned, and then, just as others might cry, she bursts into laughter. The surfers have lost their appetite for her, for the joke, and have returned to talking about the killer waves. They ignore her as she makes her way back to our table.

"Did you see that?" Lucy asks Tara. "I haven't lost it." She slumps back into her seat.

The sun fades, and the waitress lights some electric tiki torches inside the thatched hut bar. I take off my Italian sunglasses and set them on the table.

A strong young Samoan man with a tattooed armband approaches our table and pulls up a chair. "*Malo,*" he says, greeting Lucy, whom he seems to know. The young man turns his attention to me. "You're American?" he asks, flashing a smile the same dingy white as the big shark's tooth around his neck, a talisman surfers wear to protect them from sharks.

The waitress delivers three more big Vailimas. She eyes me. "Be careful with these," she whispers, glancing around the table, but I wave on another beer. I can take care of myself. I study Tara and Lucy, who are joking about sex and boyfriends to cover up the loneliness in their lives stretching out in front of them like the endless sea. I knock over my beer, and it drips all over my sandals and dress. It's sticky and I need air.

"I'm going over there," I say, pointing to the ocean and pushing back from the table. "Splash some water." I walk away in the sand, and the fa'afafine nod, barely registering. Their heads are low to the table, whispering to each other.

"Me, too," says the Samoan surfer, following, and I don't care, whatever. I wander by some camping huts to the edge of the water, dip my feet in, and wash away the beer. I look up at the stars, so bright, and a wave comes up, startling me, pushing me onto my seat, my dress now sopping and sandy.

"Here," says the Samoan man, taking my hand and pulling me up. How nice that he's helping.

"Look." I gesture at my dress helplessly. "Look what happened." He keeps my hand in his, pulling me away from the water, pulling me along the beach.

I drop his hand. "Stay there," I command and giggle and go to the other side of some brush to pee. I lift my skirt and squat; it's hard to balance when you've had a few drinks. Men have it easy. Emerging from the bush, I don't see the surfer guy, which is good. I just need to sit, to breathe, I don't feel so good. Sit awhile and then find some water to drink.

There's the surfer guy, coming toward me. He sits down, and then he is too close. "Baby, I want you," he says out of the blue and puts an arm around me. Where did he get that line, this silly surfer? I push him away.

"I want to lick you," the Samoan guy says, more urgently, and he starts pawing around. "Go away," I say, pushing him more strongly.

I start to get up, and he pushes me down into the sand. "Really," I say, angry now. "Leave me alone."

"I want to fuck you, baby."

"No!" He is ridiculous. I make a mighty effort to get up, and he puts his hand on my hip to keep my down. Red alarms go off in my head, and I summon all my will, my strength, that bolt of energy to fight him off, and his hand pushes harder on my hip bone and he laughs at me, drunkenly enjoying the game. He still thinks I want to kiss him, fucking moron. No, I say, turning my head into the sand and closing my eyes. No.

I WAKE UP, curled in a fetal position. I have no idea how much time has passed. I brush sand from my mouth and look to see if the Samoan guy has gone. I push myself up to sitting and then lean over again. I heave up everything, the beer, the pineapple. I vomit until it's bitter and my throat is raw and there is nothing left, but I can't stop heaving. I close my eyes and try to breathe in deep. Some people would not be in this situation. Some people would be back in their hut, in bed with a book. Some people would not have gotten so fucking drunk with a bunch of drag queens in Samoa. But I am an idiot, I am a mess. In the sand I notice the shark's tooth the surfer was wearing, the leather cord ripped apart.

I stand up, nearly sober, and walk back to the water's edge. After a hard wave, there is a calm pooling of water. I rinse my face, then walk into the warm water in my dress, dunking my head, swimming under, washing everything, rubbing my skin until I feel clean. When I surface, I am alert enough to realize I should get out of the water. I wish I had a towel.

Back to the bar, Tara and Lucy are still at the table, their heads resting on their arms on the table. I tap them, and it takes a few minutes for them to register my presence. "There you are," says Tara, rousing herself.

"Did you go for a little swim?" Lucy asks. "Did the surfer make you all wet?" Lucy laughs, but Tara notices my pale face and straightens up.

I locate my beach bag and go into the restroom, where I rinse my face and cup my hands to drink as much water as I can. I change into my sarong, clean again.

"Let's go," I say, back at the table.

"School tomorrow," Tara says, struggling to her feet, giving her head a shake to get rid of the drunkenness.

Turning to leave, I remember something. "My sunglasses!" I search the table, my bag, and turn to Lucy. "Did you see my sunglasses? They were right here on the table." Those were my favorite sunglasses. I found them in Rome, paid more for them than anyone should pay for shoes, much less sunglasses, but they'd been worth it, they were cool, women stopped me on the street to ask where I got those sunglasses. And now some drunk fa'afafine bitch has them hiding in her pockets. "Fuck!" I say, and Tara looks away, embarrassed.

It is not Tara's fault. Forget it. But my favorite sunglasses. They're gone.

"Let's go," I say, wishing we could leave Lucy behind. We speed back toward Lucy's plantation and drop her off without saying good-bye. I slow down when it's just Tara in the car, and she's apologizing for the glasses, for their drunkenness, and I reassure her, no, no, it's all fine. When I get to Tara's village, the open-sided house, I can see the sleeping forms of her mother and father in the corner on the mats. I say good-bye to Tara, and then offer her the wet dress in my bag, which I never want to see again. "It needs a wash," I say, "but it might fit you."

"*Fa'afetei*," says Tara and gives me a gentle hug.

*   *   *

WHEN I FINALLY get out of bed in the morning, I stumble as
I stand up. I rub the crease where my hip meets my leg, tender
and sore deep inside. I must have strained it somehow. My head
is pounding. I stand under the lukewarm shower until I am as
awake as I'm going to get.

Coffee will help. I walk over to the main house and sit on the
porch. The view of the waves is soothing.

A van of surfers pulls up. The driver's tanned arm, leaning out the window, has a tattoo around it. My stomach jumps.
The Samoan surfer climbs out of the van with some tourists,
chatty New Zealanders, who are climbing the stairs to the
porch. I want to bolt, but there's no way to leave without walking straight past them. I put my head down and hide my face
behind my coffee cup, wishing for my sunglasses. I will myself invisible as they settle into their table. I think I'm safe and
then sense something or someone standing in front of me. The
waiter with breakfast. I lift my head, and it's the surfer. I cover
my face with my hand and pretend it is a bad hallucination that
will go away.

"I'm sorry," I hear him say, and I cannot speak. I'm frozen,
still as an animal whose only defense is to blend into the background. After a couple of beats, he moves, I hear him go down
the stairs, and then, in the distance, the van door opening and
closing.

I get up to settle my bill. I can't eat breakfast, I have got to
catch my plane. In a moment I'm driving away.

When I climb the stairs to the plane, my hip twinges sharply. I take my seat in the cramped plane and suddenly feel there isn't enough air, the space is too enclosed. I close my eyes and breathe slowly. After the plane takes off, I peer out at the island, at its sultry greenness, and at the Falealupo Peninsula, the edge of the earth, entrance to the underworld with its evil spirits.

Chapter Six

HOUSTON * KANSAS CITY *
SAN FRANCISCO

2002

Home from Samoa, I unpack my bag and gather my clothes to throw everything into the laundry. When I touch the green flowered sarong I wore the last night on Savai'i, I drop the whole bundle on the floor. I throw the sarong in the trash—to get rid of the whole episode, it never existed—and go take a shower, even though I already had one that morning.

In just a few days, I'm packing again, back at the airport, boarding a plane to Houston. I'm suddenly exhausted from traveling, going through the motions, looking over my shoulder, nervous. I want to be home, but I don't want to be home alone.

In Texas, I'm doing a prison story. At a coffee shop I meet an ex-con, the kind with tattooed tears by his eyes for the number of people he's killed, and have to take notes as fast as I can to keep him from seeing how my hand is shaking. I pretend I need a third cup of coffee just so I don't have to walk out with him, then wait until his pickup truck is a speck in the distance before I leave, driving in the other direction. In the rental car, I get disoriented and panicky and have to pull over several times to check the map and breathe.

I head to Huntsville, sweltering in the brick red heat, to interview a prisoner. Waiting outside the watchtower with its rolls of razor wire, getting buzzed in and inspected, I know I'm probably safer here than anywhere else, but still. They always make you sign that clause saying it's not their fault if you're held hostage and they won't do anything to help you if you are. When I sit down to interview a young man, in for murder for a hate crime, he is behind a mesh screen, which makes it even more unsettling. The only way to look at him, to make any contact, is to look directly into his pupils, the tiny area inside the screen mesh, which is too intense. I spend my entire time in Texas apprehensive and afraid. It's unlike me; I've been to prisons before, I've interviewed someone with Charles Manson sitting at the next table over and kept my cool.

Barely home again, I go to Kansas City, the home of Hallmark Cards, and stay at a chain hotel, as bland and benign a place as you can imagine, to report a story about a divorcée in her fifties who became HIV-positive the first time she slept with another man after twenty-five years of marriage. She was faithful all those years, and the first time she had a fling after her divorce, her first taste of freedom, she paid for it dearly. She's a former reporter herself, upbeat and intelligent, telling a brave tale, but she is also lonely and frightened. After we have dinner, it occurs to me back in the hotel room that I don't have anyone to call at home, the phone would just ring.

Her story fills me with another kind of anxiety, and by the time I touch down in San Francisco, I'm fretting that I could be HIV-positive or have some other disease. I call around, frantic, until I find a clinic that can take me right away to be tested and drive to a far suburb for an exam. When I explain out loud to the nurse practitioner why I need all the tests, the memory of it hits me and I feel queasy. She reassures me and says I'm probably fine (which turns out to be the case). I am relieved that at least I will know. I stop off at a mall on the way back home and buy an expensive pair of Italian sunglasses to replace the ones I lost. I put them on, and things start to look a little better again.

AT HOME I feel more urgency than ever to have someone near me, to feel settled. For the first time in my life, I feel that I need, not just want, someone who can look out for me. I am nervous on my own, even walking in the evening around the Haight Ashbury, where I have lived, safely, without incident, for twenty years. Now all of a sudden the homeless people who have been panhandling me for years seem menacing, and the Goths and punks look more threatening than just kids playing dress-up. I take to riding my bicycle more because it's faster than walking.

I'm annoyed that I feel so fragile. I've always imagined myself invulnerable, as though I've had a feisty little guardian angel on my shoulder, and now she's flown off. I may not be as tough as I appear—my eyes glisten while interviewing people who have a difficult story to tell, when I ought to be more of a pro—but I'm usually able to present a strong front to the world. Now I don't trust that I'm not going to fall apart. I don't trust myself, period.

It's a little like when I decided to get married, to trust my heart and entire future to someone, and then was painfully betrayed: how could I ever trust myself to make a smart choice about a man again? The truth is that I've been too afraid, ever since, to even try to be in a relationship, because look what happened last time.

So how can I trust myself to travel alone again? Now I'm anxious just leaving the house. I make plans with my women friends or go out in groups. I put a whistle on my key chain. I'd like to meet a new man, someone who could walk by my side, be a companion, watch my back, but the last thing I can do is go out on a date with a stranger. I stick to my friends, whom I realize I can count on more than I thought.

When I drive down to Monterey one weekend, for instance, my car dies on the way, I'm in the middle of nowhere, and night is falling. Big black vans and Harleys slow down menacingly while passing my little car. I have a soft-top convertible that could be easily slashed and broken into. I call my friend Guillermo in Santa Cruz (we've been friends for several years and, since we have the same birthday, always celebrate by cooking for a big party together). He doesn't hesitate: he rides his motorcycle right down and sits with me in the car, talking about food, until the tow truck arrives. It freaks me out when I climb into the truck that the driver is wearing plastic examining room gloves, under which I can see the outline of a swastika tattoo. I climb right back out and tell Guillermo, who says calm down, he's an ex-skinhead freak, but we need to get the car back, I'll ride right along behind the truck. When we get back to Santa Cruz, he makes us big steak sandwiches with focaccia and caramelized onions and we drink a bottle of wine before I head to the guest room. We go body surfing the next day, and when the waves get rough, I ask him if we should be worried. "The question right now is whether it's *useful* to be worried," he says, and so we swim like mad, but I know that as long as I'm with him, I'm in no danger.

At home in San Francisco, my friend Sandra, a woman of Italian–Puerto Rican descent and temperament whom I've known for many years, drops by to catch up after my recent trips. She has shared many a glass of wine with me after I've broken up with someone or calmed my outrage or confusion after a bad date with her practical, good-hearted advice. She is married with an adopted son; at age thirty-eight, she decided she wanted a husband and family and eventually got them; she's made a lot of sacrifices for her child, as everyone does, taking full-time jobs when she'd rather be a freelance photographer, considering a move to the suburbs, where the schools are better but where she'll feel culturally stifled, but she has a clear sense of her priorities and an optimism about her circumstances.

We hug each other, and I give her a fierce-looking Samoan T-shirt for her eight-year-old son. I pour wine and recount my trips to Houston and Kansas City.

"Wait a minute," says Sandra, interrupting me after a couple of minutes. "Back up. What about Samoa? Who cares about Kansas City? I want to hear about Samoa."

I tell her the fa'afafine were interesting, the islands were lush and the beaches pristine, but the photographer I worked with was a real asshole, treating me like his photo assistant and the fa'afafine like models. "I was really pissed off, too, because I lost my favorite sunglasses."

Sandra looks at me quizzically. "You went all the way to

Samoa, and all you can say is that the photographer was an asshole and you lost your sunglasses?" She frowns. "Come on—what's the matter with you? It's Samoa! Exotic island paradise! I'd give anything to go there for ten days."

I shrug. "It was a lot of work, that's all." I wipe my eyes.

"What is it?" Sandra knows me too well.

"I had a difficult trip," I finally say. "That's all."

"What?"

I shake my head.

"You can tell me," says Sandra. She reaches over and puts her hand on my forearm.

It all comes tumbling out—my drunkenness, my stupidity, the surfer on the beach. My fear ever since, the entire summer, not wanting to be alone, not wanting to travel, not being able to trust myself. Until I said it out loud, I didn't realize I was so upset about the whole thing.

Sandra's face darkens, and when I stop, she gives me a hug and pushes strands of hair out of my wet face. It's a relief that a friend knows. Sandra gets up for a box of tissues, offers me one, wipes her own eyes, and refills our glasses.

"Shit," she says. "I'm so sorry. I don't know what to say." She heaves a sigh. "You went to the doctor?"

"I'm fine," I say. "I had all the tests." Then, suddenly, outraged: "The only place I could get an appointment right away was in San Rafael. The receptionist at *my* doctor's office, my fucking *women's health* clinic, told me it wasn't an emergency."

"*I'd* call it an emergency." Sandra is mad, too, which is satisfying.

"Don't you think?" I say. "I mean, okay, it was a couple of weeks later, but still. It hit me all of a sudden, and I was totally freaked out. I needed to deal with it right then."

"Of course," she says in a calmer voice. "Why didn't you call me?"

It's hard to explain why I didn't call her or anyone else. I was too embarrassed even to call the psychologist I used to see, so I wrote her an e-mail, which she never replied to, probably because I'd never written her one before and it went straight into her junk mail. In any case, my shrink's most memorable line to me ever was "For such a smart woman you sure are stupid about men," and this incident pretty much proved that point, just adding another dimension to my usual bad judgment. (Later, when I do tell her, she's helpful, and I realize as usual that I was projecting.)

"I don't know," I tell Sandra. "I just couldn't tell anyone I knew. I did call a crisis line, but I got one of those young women who speak like every sentence is a question? You know, 'It's not your fault? You should, like, talk to a therapist? We have re-sources? You should, like, press charges?' "

Sandra shakes her head.

"I think there should be a crisis line for people who can't speak in declarative sentences or who say 'like' every like other word," I say. "It's a complete abuse of the English language." I'm furious, suddenly, about the way people under thirty say "like" all the time. Something ought to be done. "It makes me fucking *crazy.*"

Sandra touches my shoulder. "Relax," she says. "I don't think that's worth getting so upset about." She sighs. "So, *did* you call the police?"

"Of course not," I say, reaching for another tissue. "It was Samoa. What would the police say? You shouldn't get drunk and walk around with a stranger at night on the beach, you stupid tourist? I mean, I was hanging out with the guy."

"Being drunk and stupid doesn't make it your fault."

"Well, it wouldn't have happened otherwise."

Sandra takes a sip of wine. "Are you okay? I mean physically."

"I pulled something in my hip, that's all. Ligament or something."

"Well, that's lucky."

Lucky. I wipe my face and blow my nose. "The thing is, I was *so* stupid, completely reckless, getting drunk, taking a walk with that guy."

"Hey," says Sandra, firmly. "Stop saying that. So you were partying too much. Big deal. You're impulsive and spontaneous, and you like to have a good time. That's what makes you *you.*"

"That's what got me in trouble."

"Okay, yeah, so you don't have to get so sloshed when you're out in another country, and probably you won't next time, but it might've happened anyway," Sandra says. "The last thing you need to do right now is beat yourself up."

We sit quietly for a few minutes. "In a way," I say, sighing, "it's kind of like just another bad one-night stand. I mean, I've ended up in bed with men who were using me, who didn't care about me, I've felt shitty the next day, so what's the difference?"

Sandra stares at me. "How can you say that?" She's almost yelling. "You're right, you *are* being stupid. It's an assault, okay? An attack. Samoa, wherever, he had no right. You were drunk, fine. That doesn't mean that being raped doesn't matter. That's totally crazy."

"I don't want to use that word," I say coolly. I'm not going to go through life sounding like some kind of a victim. "It's not like a stranger jumped out of the bushes with a knife. It's not like I was kidnapped and forced to sell my body on the streets. It wasn't really a big deal. I knew he wasn't going to hurt me."

"He did hurt you," Sandra says quietly.

"I'm *trying* not to be so upset about it." I wipe my eyes.

"It's okay to be upset. You *should* be upset. *I'm* upset." Sandra is waving her half-Italian hands around. She calms down and uses a big-sister tone. "Blaming yourself is not going to make it okay. You can be angry and scared, and it may keep coming back to you for a long time, and that's enough for you to deal with. I should know."

I look up at her brown eyes and deeply knit brow.

Sandra is quiet for a second. "It happened to me, too."

"You're kidding."

Sandra shakes her head. "It was a long time ago. My best friend's boyfriend, on a vacation in Florida. They were having a fight, and he came into my room to 'talk' about it. I got pissed off at him, protecting my friend. He went nuts, beating me up pretty badly. Broke my nose." She touches the ridge, which I now see is a little crooked.

"Oh, my god. Did you call the police?"

"No. My friend begged me not to."

"She was sticking up for him?" I shake my head in wonder.

"Battered girlfriend. My mistake was trying to protect her from him, to get her to leave. That's why I went along in the first place. And I blamed myself for everything."

"Why the fuck didn't you turn him in?" I say, raising my voice. "How could you blame yourself? You were just trying to protect a friend. And some *friend*. Jesus." I can't believe that happened to Sandra, who is always so cheerful, strong, and practical. Then I'm quieter. "You've never told me about it."

"I don't think about it very much. But you'd be surprised how many women you know have been raped. Once it happens to you, you hear a lot of stories. It's like you're part of a secret club. It takes a long time to get over it, and it affects people in different ways. At least I think with me it's history."

"Did it take you a long time to trust men again?"

"I had Paul, who was great. We were already together then. When I told him, he wanted to track the guy down and murder him, but he was wonderful with me. He took good care of me."

My eyes fill with tears. "I think it's going to be a long time before I can deal with men again," I say.

"Maybe," says Sandra. "But you can't let it get you down for too long. You have to get your sense of power back. You had a bad experience, but you're still you, you're still strong." She rubs my arm. "Look, you'll get over this. Just concentrate on doing little things that make you feel better right now. Take baths, eat good food, go to yoga. You don't have to go traipsing around the world by yourself. Okay?"

"Okay," I say, attempting a smile. I refill our glasses. We're quiet for a few minutes. "You know," I finally say, "The thing that pisses me off is that I was having such a great time in Samoa, it was such a high. There were gorgeous beaches, I found this amazing warm pool with a waterfall to swim in, and a perfect little hotel run by Italians."

"There you go. Focus on the waterfall." Sandra raises her glass. "To forgetting about this," she says. "And that surfer? Shark bait."

I can see his shark's tooth necklace in the sand. I pulled so hard I ripped it off his neck. "To the sharks." We clink glasses.

I head to Nevada for several weeks and stay at my friend Maya's ranch, away from the world, a place I've loved to visit since I befriended her daughter fifteen years ago, when we drove around the state doing a political story for *Vogue,* interviewing showgirls, ranchers, prostitutes, and casino workers. Since then her daughter has gotten married and had two children, and has a lot less time to roam around, but she is one of my few married friends who still includes me as family and who makes time for us to take walks on our own. There is plenty of space on the ranch, with its wide-open view of the plains, and the only thing I have to be afraid of is catching a mouse and having to reset the snappy trap.

I wake up each morning and sit in the hot tub with Maya, who comments on the pink-streaked sky and mentions that a coyote went skulking through the pasture right before dawn. Then, at nearly ninety, she dips into the cold pool, and I, at half her age, have no choice but to splash in after her, shivering awake and ready for strong coffee. She dresses, and we go inside where she begins to knead her sourdough bread. I go off to spend the day writing and hiking in the hills behind the ranch with a big dog by my side. In the evening, after a swim, I chop vegetables, drink wine, and talk about politics with Maya and whichever of her diverse friends has arrived from distant parts for dinner.

Maya has a lot to discuss, since she's lived quite a life. After her divorce in the 1970s, which seemed to light a fire under her, she became passionately involved in political causes, from welfare rights to Central America, supporting grassroots movements, particularly those organized by women; along the way she ran for the U.S. Senate. After her husband left and her children grew up, she expanded her family to include taking care of the wider world, and in return, so many people look after her. She lives modestly on her ranch, for all the money she gives away, and doesn't travel much anymore, but she enjoys hearing about my trips.

She has created a wonderful atmosphere in her old age, surrounded by friends. The ranch is self-contained, full of calm and simple pleasures, with people always within shouting distance if you need them. It's good to stay in one place for a while, peaceful and comforting to feel part of an extended family, safe and protected and loved.

BUT I CAN'T hide out in Nevada forever.

Even back when this was a divorce ranch, the society women had to leave after six weeks of carousing with the cowboys and take the train back to New York. I have to go back to work, back out into the world, and get past my fear. Because as afraid as I suddenly am of being alone, of being hurt, violated, victimized—all the worst-case scenarios of being a single, independent woman—I am more afraid that I am going to lose touch with some essential part of who I am. I'm not sure who I would be if I were not, at heart, that kid who wanted to hop freight trains, was unafraid to walk around the cobblestone streets of San Miguel de Allende and try to chat with the locals, who idolized glamorous Brenda Starr, went three thousand miles away to college, and then set off to travel in the Mediterranean alone. I only know I would be depressed, and I am not, by nature, depressed. I have to get over this.

So I wave good-bye to Maya, put the top down, and drive over the Sierras back to San Francisco. It is one of the few times, at home, when I wish I had a regular job to get up and go to every morning, instead of trying to engage in the optimistic and uncertain business of coming up with ideas and stories and trying to sell them. I pitch a bunch of article ideas, none of them quite right, nothing moving, until one day an editor calls and asks if I could please do a quick story about bicycling in Provence, focusing on the food and bringing along a female friend who also likes to ride. This is one of those moments when you scrub and scrub and then a fairy godmother appears and waves her magic wand. Of course I'd like to go to Provence with a friend, in safe company.

Because I'm still feeling nervous about traveling, I ask someone very familiar and comfortable, whom I've known my whole life, to come along—my cousin Charlotte, who is an extraordinary cook and speaks perfect French. I know she will be as eager as I am to sample the ratatouille, tapenade, figs, pastries, and wines of the region, to taste the simple, rich pleasures of a cuisine that Roger Vergé, one of the greatest chefs of the south of France, describes as "gay, healthful, and natural, gathering together the gifts of the soil like an armful of wildflowers."

Arriving in the center of Avignon by train from Paris is like stepping out of a high-tech transportation corridor into a medieval fairy tale, with fourteenth-century stone palaces and narrow, winding streets. Charlotte greets me at the hotel with a bottle of Côtes du Rhône to inaugurate our trip. From the start, it turns out to be a comfort to travel with someone I've known my whole life and a pleasure to expand not only our relationship but also my understanding of all things French. Whereas I speak only a few phrases, Charlotte is fluent; though I can appreciate an extraordinary meal, she can dissect its ingredients and technique.

In the morning, we wander around, stepping out onto the Pont d'Avignon bridge that stretches over just half the Rhône. We could admire the town's imposing palaces and whimsical shop windows all morning, but our noses lead us to the market instead. There, we are overwhelmed by the baskets of baby vegetables, bunches of fragrant lavender and thyme, mounds of olives and capers, and perfect rounds of cheese. We buy a few ripe figs and then meander to a pâtisserie, where we savor a flaky pastry stuffed with spinach and goat cheese. Charlotte is so knowledgeable about French food that I nickname her "Cousine Cuisine."

We meet up with our group in the morning and begin our cycling in a tiny hilltop town, Crillon-le-Brave, which has a splendid view of Mont Ventoux, the bald-headed mountain that dominates the region (and that the poet Petrarch climbed in 1335, becoming the first person in recorded history to go mountain climbing for fun). The hotel is a collection of centuries-old stone houses cobbled together with lush pocket gardens. When we check into our suite, Charlotte opens the latches on the windows overlooking the villages and valley below, then twirls around the room. "Okay," she says, clapping her hands, "I'm happy."

We take a warm-up spin around the Plateau de Vaucluse, where the fields are thick with lavender. As we ride side by side on the empty country roads, catching up, I realize that Charlotte is as anxious as I am to get back in touch with something deep, true, and unafraid about herself. This is Charlotte's first trip since her daughter, who is three, was born. She both revels in the freedom to be in adult company—which I take for granted—and aches for her little girl. Since childhood, Charlotte, a petite strawberry blonde, has always been a dynamo—a gymnastics champ, ballerina, concert pianist, artist, caterer, competitive runner. She's entirely focused, and it seems there's nothing she can't do well. But the birth of her daughter brought her low, bluer than she's ever been, and ever since she's had bouts of feeling guilty about being depressed when she has such a darling baby, out of touch with her athletic body, her identity lost, feeling trapped in the house, uncertain of her future. Cycling in the Provençal countryside seems to restore us both to our stronger selves, at least out there in the lavender fields.

And so does the food. At a picnic lunch with the world's best baguettes, olives, tapenade, fresh fromage de chèvre, and charcuterie meats, we regretfully refuse the local rosé wine since we want to finish the ride. "This is going to be the most difficult decision of the trip," Charlotte says, eyeing the bottle, "whether to drink the wine at lunch."

Charlotte and I make a great team: we both love bicycling between villages and coming back to our posh medieval-era hotels exhausted and hungry. We finish a long day of bicycling and climbing hills with a six-course French meal and a view of the sun setting fiery red over the hills. We lose everything but the moment as we eat lobster in a tomato shell; pan-roasted fois gras with peppered toast and wine sauce; roasted pigeon with ginger, white beans, and tomato; local cheese; roasted figs with cinnamon crème brûlée, everything finished off with a warm and crunchy chocolate parcel. It's a memorable dinner.

But the meal we enjoy most is the next day, and much simpler. We ride past silvery olive trees through the Calavon Valley, landing at a bistro in the tidy, picturesque hill town of Eygalières. There, under an outdoor grape arbor, we eat a tangy goat cheese melted on toast, niçoise pizza, runny chocolate cake, and a chilled pear soup. "Now, this," says Charlotte, sighing, "is real Provençal food."

When we start in on our first glass of wine, I realize that even though I am here in paradise, I have not felt entirely happy since the day I floated under the waterfall in Samoa. Our first course arrives, the wine warms our cheeks, and we gasp at the freshness of the flavors, so transporting that my eyes start to water.

"What is it?" Charlotte asks. I don't want to tell her that I haven't been myself lately and that this is the first time since then that I've started to feel a tingle, a deep, warm sense of everything being all right again. I forget about the power of food, friendship, and family to revive and comfort me. I don't want to say all this out loud; to talk about my new sense of vulnerability would put too much of a burden on her, on the trip, and it's something I want to forget entirely for the moment. Instead, I simply say how wonderful the meal is and how it reminds me of another meal I had a few years ago.

At home, I tell Charlotte, I keep a framed photo of myself clinking glasses with a friend at dinner. It's not flattering: I look wan and worn out, with red-rimmed eyes, cheeks flushed. But the expression the camera caught is one of pure contentment. The photo was taken on May 8, 1997. I remember the date because on May 7, my husband left me. Up until dinner, May 8 was prob- ably the worst day of my life. I spent most of it in bed, trying to grasp my new reality, that the man I had loved and married and planned to have children with had left me, abruptly, for some- one else. I'd been lied to, cheated on, and abandoned, and I had a dinner reservation at Chez Panisse in Berkeley, the restaurant Alice Waters made famous for its local farm-to-table approach and simple presentation of exceptional ingredients.

Ironically, the dinner with my longtime friend Larry was pay- ment for a bet I'd lost about which of us would get married first. We'd made the wager years before, when I'd thought I was too free-spirited to settle down, before I met the man who changed my mind. After I wed, Larry got married, too, and each of our lives got busier. Finally, our schedules coincided with a day we could get a reservation. That it turned out to be the day after my husband left me made me laugh at the universe in spite of my sadness.

When I told Larry the news, he asked if I wanted to cancel

dinner. But I needed a reason to get out of bed, and that day, dinner at my favorite restaurant was the only one that would work. I might cry through every course, but I was going.

I met Larry at the entryway to the dark-wood Arts & Crafts building, greeted by a spray of wildflowers and a large bowl of fruit in season. We were seated in a cozy corner, with a view of the kitchen and its copper plates. We started with a glass of champagne and a plate of Hog Island oysters on the half shell with little sausages. The oysters were so fresh they tasted like my tears. I closed my eyes to feel the sensation of the sea.

Larry chatted about wine with the server, chose something French, and started telling me about novels he'd enjoyed recently. He knew better than to ask how I was feeling.

After the oysters came a fish and shellfish soup, with a delicate broth of fennel and leeks. The flavors were so subtle and perfectly balanced that my mind had to close off everything else to rest on my taste buds. There was no room in my consciousness for heartbreak, divorce, and having to move out of my house, only space for a soup whose flavors shimmered like gold.

The server poured a dark-hued Bandol wine, ripe and inviting. The flavors spread across my mouth into a smile. The main course arrived, an earthy grilled duck breast with rhubarb sauce and roasted turnips. The rhubarb took me back to my childhood, when I would pick the bitter stalks from my grandmother's garden and we would make my favorite pink stew. Grandma is gone, but rhubarb is as permanent as my memories of her. The rhubarb duck comforted me with its familiarity; no matter what happens, in spring there is always rhubarb.

When dessert came, a berry feuilleté, perfect little fresh spring berries in the lightest and flakiest of pastry, Larry uttered a French expression of delight. He said the meal made up for the time, years before, when we'd gone bicycling on Thanksgiving when everything was closed and all we could find for dinner was mango juice and pretzels. At that moment, the Chez Panisse meal was making up for so much more. The server snapped our photo as we finished our wine.

I would go back to my tears the next day, and it would be months before such a look of contentment would cross my face again. But at that moment, sharing a wonderful meal with a friend, the last pastry flake melting on my tongue like snow, I was happy. And every time I looked at that photo during the dark times that followed, I knew I would be happy again.

"I guess it's silly to talk about a French meal in the States when we're here eating the real thing," I say. Charlotte smiles. She gestures to the waiter, brings out her camera, puts her arm around me, and asks him to take our photo.

WHEN THE CYCLING trip finishes, we take a train to Paris, finishing off chocolates we found in Saint-Rémy on the way, each infused with a hint of Provence—lavender, thyme, basil. When we arrive in Paris, Charlotte is prepared, having already researched the restaurants and found us a charming and inexpensive hotel. I've been to Paris only a couple times before, the last time for a few days with my mother, who wanted to travel in Europe with me to help take my mind off my divorce, on the way to Italy.

Paris is the perfect place for cheering you up, almost by example; its sublime beauty lights up all that gray.

I call the Professor to let him know I'm in town; I've never spent any time with him on his home turf, so I'm excited and nervous to see him. I also don't know how he is going to feel, hearing from me out of the blue. When he answers the phone, he is surprised and then delighted that I'm in Paris, and wants to see me right away.

Charlotte and I meet him in a perfect French café, and since I'm with my cousin, he is formal, kissing us both on both cheeks, but then hugging me tight. When we pull away, I notice that for the first time since I've known him he's wearing a tie, an old-fashioned red plaid thing, instead of his usual scarf. I wonder if he dresses more conventionally at home in Paris than when he's traveling, being his Mediterranean self, and then I notice something else about the tie.

"The Fraser tartan," I say, and laugh; it's the dress plaid from my family's Scottish clan. The Professor is pleased that I've noticed, and I'm happy he thought of me in Scotland, even though we're no longer lovers, and wanted to surprise me the next time he saw me. It's funny that while in Scotland, he went looking for my ancestral home, made a point of it, though I've never stepped foot in that country.

"There are Frasers everywhere in Inverness," he reports. "But none of them at all like you." He smiles at me with his crooked French teeth and watery blue eyes. "They're very serious, very hard people. I think you must have an Italian bastard somewhere in your past." He gives me a little squeeze.

*   *   *

WE HAVE ONLY part of a day together; he has a girlfriend and responsibilities with his children. But for a few fine hours he shows me his Paris, a relaxed stroll through the Tuileries, then secret courtyards, and along the Seine. He takes me to lunch in a restaurant he's frequented since his student days, a grand old place with huge antique mirrors that retains the marvelous atmosphere, amid its splendor, of being a dive. The Professor points out slots in the walls where the regulars used to keep their cloth napkins. "This has been here since the time of Balzac," he says.

He shows me his apartment, a tiny place in the Sixteenth Arrondissement, a more bourgeois neighborhood, he explains, than he's used to, but he's here because his kids and their mother live nearby. It's a small studio dominated by a big desk, with books floor to ceiling, and a little nook with Indian pillows where he sleeps; there is little room for anything here but his mind. There are a couple of beautiful drawings and a photo of a woman, his girlfriend presumably, crossing her slender ankles and wearing white pumps. I do not imagine the Professor with someone who wears white pumps.

We have little time, because he has to go pick up his son. It's so different from all our other visits together, where the days stretched out long, with no plans except to decide when and where to eat, to swim now or later. We have so much to say to each other, but, conscious of our short time, we sit there on his couch, saying nothing. Finally I ask him about the book he's writing, and he gives me an enthusiastic description, verging on academic; it'll be his best book yet, he thinks, and will even be translated into English. "Now you can read *my* book," he says.

He asks where I have traveled, and I tell him Italy, Samoa, Tahiti, Nicaragua. "Ah," he says, "*la bella vita* continues. You are always on the road."

"I'm not settled down like you," I say, half teasing, glancing at the photograph of the woman in white shoes.

"It's not what I expected," he says. "But I'm happier with a woman, someone to share dinner with." He sighs. "My secret now is that I have no secret life. My students look at me like I'm an old man. I'm completely boring."

"Never," I say.

"*Grazie, signorina,*" he says, and strokes the back of my hand.

He asks about my next trip, and I say I'm not sure, I may take a little break from traveling.

"Because you have a boyfriend?"

I shake my head no. "I'm not interested in men right now."

"Impossible," he says. "No men, no travel? What's happened to you?"

I get up and pretend to inspect the art books in his library. Then I sit back down. We are so used to touching each other, and now we can't touch at all. Tears start to roll down my eyes.

"*Che c'è?*" he asks. What is it?

"I miss you," I tell him in Italian. "I miss knowing that I'll see you."

He picks up my hand, squeezes it, then gives me a hug. I use his Egyptian scarf to wipe my eyes and pull away.

"Do you know what I liked best about your book?" he asks.

I shake my head no. We have never spoken much about the fact that I wrote a book about our romance.

"It was the first time I understood that you loved me."

I nod yes, unable to speak.

"We've had a beautiful story," he says. "Life is full of stories, and we'll have more, each of us. Though maybe fewer." He smiles.

"*Sì*," I say. He embraces me again and then kisses me and then caresses me, and I pull away, alarmed.

"I can't," I say and start crying afresh.

"It's nothing. Just a little caress," he says, opening his hands wide. "We are old friends."

"It's not that," I say, and somehow I tell him that I don't feel comfortable touching anyone at all, I can't travel, I'm too afraid, something bad happened to me in Samoa. He listens to me and frowns. He brings out one of his little cigars, in a tin box, and lights it, inhaling. "Do you want one?" he asks.

I shake my head. "I only smoked that one time, in Ischia."

He blows a perfect smoke ring, and in spite of myself I smile.

He considers my story. "*Mi dispiace molto,*" he says, giving me a hug and then still holding on to my hand. "I'm so sorry. I'm sorry that happened to you, my dear." He takes another puff. "But don't make things too complicated. That experience happened, and of course you always want to be careful. But you can't let one experience with a cretin change you. You're a stronger woman than that." He strokes my hair. "You love to travel, you have a great big appetite for life, and that's who you are. You just have to continue to be yourself. It's simple."

"Simple," I repeat. "Okay, Professor."

He holds up his glass. "*La bella vita,*" he says. I pick up my glass, a little shaky, and clink. He gathers his coat and bag, and then he walks with me to the Métro.

I SPEND ANOTHER couple days in Paris with Charlotte, wandering the streets, visiting museums, eating long lunches, and finding little shopping areas. With all the beautiful clothes and jewelry, we are still mainly interested in food; the only things we buy are mustards and salts from a gourmet shop on Île-St.-Louis. On our last day, we're on a busy street near a bookstore, and I see a familiar figure emerge, with his curls and scarf. Out of everyone in Paris, I randomly run into the Professor on the street. I walk up to him and shake my head wordlessly.

He kisses me on both cheeks. "*Incroyable,*" he says. "You see? We keep meeting each other." He glances at his watch.

"*Ciao,*" I say. Hello and good-bye. *Ciao, ciao.*

"*Ciao, Laura,*" he says, pulling away. "*Ciao, bella. Ci vediamo.*" We'll see each other.

I WISH IT were as simple as the Professor made it sound, to just be my strong self and start traveling again. But I've had one good trip with my cousin, so I feel I can venture out again as long as I'm not alone.

On the way home, I stop off in New York to break up the trip and call Gustavo. He is busy but glad to hear from me, and one evening he takes me to a Brazilian restaurant, where we eat big chunks of meat, drink hearty red wine, and talk about movies. The restaurant is cozy and warm, and he speaks to the owner in Portuguese. He touches me affectionately, the way Brazilians do. We go back to where I'm staying, and I'm glad to feel that same chemistry, drawn to his irresistible sexiness. We kiss, but he can't understand why I keep pulling away, repeatedly getting up to get a glass of water or use the bathroom. I don't want to tell him, it seems like too much information, too intimate—strangely, for all that we've been intimate—but then I finally stammer out that I haven't felt comfortable with men since I was sexually assaulted several months ago. I say "sexually assaulted" as a euphemism but hate that it takes so many more syllables to say.

"I'm sorry about that," says Gustavo and touches my cheek. I'm glad he isn't reacting as though it's a huge horrible deal, the way a couple of my women friends did. "But I think—what's the expression you use in English?" he asks, his big brown eyes searching mine. Then he has it. "I think you better get back up on the horse." And then he pulls me toward him, puts his familiar arms around me, safe, holds me tight for a moment, and starts kissing me again. I let myself go; I do want to get back to being myself, to feeling sexy, to being able to make love, to trust. Even though I know I'm not going to be with Gustavo in the long run—and maybe because of that, because there is no great emotional risk—I feel comfortable with him, with his animal self, who finds the animal within me again, who wakens her and plays with her and strokes her softly until morning.

*   *   *

IN MAY, ANOTHER opportunity to go to Italy falls into my lap; *Gourmet* wants me to write a story about the cuisine of my favorite islands in the world, the Aeolians, the archipelago north of Sicily. This is a dream assignment, but I'm hesitant. A year after my trip to Samoa, I still do not want to travel by myself, even in a country I know well, where I speak the language. I'm uncomfortable, too, with the idea of eating at all those restaurants by myself. You can't enjoy meals in Italy so much if you eat alone, the food doesn't taste as good. And I'm conflicted about returning to a place where I had a romantic love affair.

There are some places to which you should probably never return. The Professor mentioned that to me several years ago, when we were on a boat to the Aeolian Islands, watching the volcano on Stromboli blowing smoke into the dawn like an Italian lighting his first cigarette of the morning. The Professor had climbed the volcano years before and never wanted to go back, for fear that the lines of tourists with their headlamps and walking sticks would forever mar the memory of his astonishing overnight trip to the edge of the erupting crater. "But you must go," he told me, blowing a few smoke rings himself. "Absolutely."

I did climb Stromboli on that trip, with a couple of amusing Italian men I met on a hydrofoil zipping between the islands. After a steep and rocky hike to the summit, we watched as molten red lava spewed into the sunset and rolled down the mountain, crashing into the ocean with a hissing boom. It's a sight I'm forever grateful I didn't miss. But walking down in the twilight, I knew, as the Professor had, that I'd probably never want to make that trek again. And now I'm not sure I want to return to the Aeolians at all.

I call my friend Giovanna in Bologna. I met her when she was doing a house trade in San Francisco ten years ago; I visited her in Bologna, and she came back and stayed with me for a month, nothing an Italian considers an imposition—really, a favor to a single friend. Giovanna would cook dinner every night, making dishes I didn't think were possible with American ingredients; it was only when I visited her in Bologna that I realized the dishes could taste even better, just from ingredients grown on Italian soil.

I mention the story idea to Giovanna, the fact that a magazine is going to pay my way to the islands, we can share a hotel room, and they'll take care of all the meals with a friend. Then I launch into how I'm not sure I should go, if it will spoil the memory to return, how I'm not really up for a trip by myself.

"*Dai*," she interrupts me. Come on. "*Andiamoci!*" she says. Let's go!

And so I find myself once again in Naples, to meet Giovanna at the dock, where the hydrofoil will take us to the islands. Giovanna, a Giulietta Masina lookalike with the same impish flair, shows up with eggplant-colored hair, orange jeans, and a bright pink sarong for me to wear on the islands. We greet each other in a flurry of kisses on each other's cheeks.

When the hydrofoil slows down and the islands first come into view, they look dry and inhospitable; they are desolate places where all living things—figs, capers, apricots, rabbits—struggle so for survival that they are bursting with the intense fragrances and flavors of a brief but concentrated life. Suddenly I am hungry: for the spicy perfume of pale pink caper flowers, for fish that swim in turquoise waters, for sweet cherry tomatoes that explode in your mouth like Stromboli, for pasta with fennel and sardines.

We spot the island of Stromboli, its whitewashed houses stacked up by the port. I don't want to mar the magnificent memory of that place, so we don't disembark. I remember Stromboli's charm, though—its narrow streets and its nervous atmosphere in the shadow of the volcano. And then there's the carnation-colored house with its plaque commemorating the place where Ingrid Bergman and Roberto Rossellini had an affair while filming *Stromboli*. (Previously, Anna Magnani, who had been living with Rossellini and had been promised the lead, overturned a bowl of bucatini with red sauce on his head before fleeing with the crew to another island, Vulcano, to make an equally forgettable film by that name.)

If there were a plaque somewhere in the Aeolians to commemorate a love affair of my own, it would be on Filicudi, one of the remotest and most desolate islands. There, for ten days, I stayed with the French professor in a white house at the top of a steep hill overlooking the port and the other craggy islands beyond. We did nothing but read, swim, make love, and decide where we wanted to eat that day. I always voted for Villa La Rosa, for the pasta of wild fennel fronds and sardines, which tasted exactly like the island's aromatic sea breeze. As with Stromboli, Filicudi is a place where I can't return, for fear of spoiling the memory of those magical days. Those days with the Professor were too perfect, that relationship too precious; I don't want to touch it, to pretend that you can have everything in life over and over again, but preserve it in the amber of memory.

That still leaves five other islands to explore, though, each with a unique personality. Panarea attracts chic Italians and honeymooners but is all tranquillity in the off-season. Lipari is the largest and most industrialized island, with a fascinating museum filled with relics from all the ships that have sunk in these violent seas since before the first Greek settlers arrived. Salina is sleepy and agricultural, covered with vineyards that bear grapes for the region's distinctive Malvasia wine. Vulcano, the island closest to Sicily, is heavily touristed on its hot-bubbling shores, but up the mountain's uplands are home to pastures that yield some of the world's best ricotta cheese. Small, outlying Alicudi has no cars and few tourist facilities—really, nothing at all.

On my last visit, all I wanted to do on the islands with the Professor was what the Italians consider an art, *far niente*—do nothing. Giovanna isn't content to far niente on the islands; she wants to explore all the tastes, sights, and activities I missed before. "*Zampetta, zampetta,*" she says, meaning "A little paw here and a little paw there, and we'll try everything." *Va bene.*

For several days, Giovanna and I explore the beaches and hills of Panarea, then eat our way around Lipari. At one, we have an exquisite caponata; in another, a fish stew made with tomatoes, capers, and dried bread. Yet for all those good meals, a corner of my hunger remains unsatisfied. I haven't tasted pasta with fennel fronds and sardines yet. Nor will I find the dish I want on Lipari. For that, we would have to go to Filicudi.

As we check the hydrofoil schedules for the next day, I am reluctant to return to Filicudi still, but I am more afraid that I will never taste that fennel pasta at Villa La Rosa again.

When we get to the island, to my relief, nothing has changed—its rocky beaches and hills terraced with ancient stone walls are still there. We rent kayaks to explore the island and, carefully navigating a jellyfish soup, come across a blue grotto. Occasionally, on some invisible cue, two thousand tiny, silvery fish arc into the air. We paddle back, ravenous, and hike the steep path cutting up the side of the hill, to Villa La Rosa perched above.

"*Magnifico,*" Giovanna says when we pause to catch our breath and stare out at the sea. Finally at the villa, we sit at a cool table on the airy, colorful terrace. The waiter warns us that they have only two pasta dishes that day. One with almonds—I hold my breath—and maccheroncini ai finocchietto. "It's made from the wild fennel growing around here," the waiter explains. Ahh.

The aroma arrives first, the sardines of the sea mixed with the fennel fronds of the island. With the plate in front of me, I pause, my desire mixed with a fear of disappointment. But the pasta is perfectly al dente, with grated bread crumbs on top and a few raisins peeking out; the fennel fronds and sardines have a wild, simple taste that satisfies me to the soul. I offer Giovanna a bite, but she refuses. "That is your pasta," she says. "And this is your island." Of the seven, she herself would pick Panarea.

I am in the very restaurant where I realized my affair with the Professor would come to an end, when he told me I was the perfect woman for vacation and left "not forever" unsaid. But right now, no trace of sadness lingers. The Professor and I had a wonderful time, and now I have the good luck to be back with a dear friend, having that same exquisite pasta, made from the same fennel fronds growing all around outside, perfuming the air. Even the wine tastes like the dry, herbal breeze. After the pasta comes grilled totano, a tender, savory giant of a squid stuffed with crunchy, olive oil–baked bread crumbs. And then a couple of perfect apricots from a tree. There should be a plaque up at Villa La Rosa, for the best lunch I've ever eaten.

I'm content here with my friend, the atmosphere, and our lunch; content for the first time in the year since I was in Samoa, in the two years since I turned forty. *La bella vita* continues in life if you let it, whatever the circumstances, and you don't have to be with a man the whole time to enjoy yourself. It's sweet to be with a lover, to be sure, but there's nothing wrong with being with one of your best friends, enjoying one of the most satisfying meals of your life, out tasting what the world has to offer, *chiacchierando,* chatting the way only women can.

"So," says Giovanna, "tell me about your boyfriends."

"No boyfriends," I say, ordering an espresso. "I have been going on a few dates here and there."

"You always say that, and then you tell me about four different men who are crazy about you," she says, pressing her fingers together in front of her. "You always have something simmering on the stove."

"Not right now. Right now I'm happy to be here." I gesture at the view of the sea.

"*Giusto,*" she says. That's right.

"I mean, I suppose you can always find someone to go out with if you want to," I say. "It's about whether or not you want to."

Giovanna bursts out laughing. "So the situation is not desperate."

"There are always all kinds of stories," I say. "For me, more short stories than novels." I tell her I've had a few fun dates, but nothing ever felt quite right.

"*È così,*" she says. It's like that.

"Lately I've been feeling like I want someone more stable, someone who will stick around. It's the first time in my life I've wanted a man around so he could take care of me, give me *protezione.*" I don't explain to her why I need to feel protected; I'm just glad I can even talk about dating again.

Our espressos arrive. Giovanna recently broke up with her husband, a big, clever, narcissistic personality who had likely been cheating on her for years. (Once when I was staying with them, Giovanna went to pick up friends at the airport; he looked at his watch, said, "We've got half an hour," with a sexy smile, adjusted his pants, and, though he was kidding, I knew he would've been happy for me to take it seriously.) Giovanna is fairly upbeat, though it hasn't been easy. She spends most of her time with her family and wide circle of female friends. She tells me she's ready to start seeing other men.

"Are you ever afraid of getting involved with someone new because you don't trust yourself not to make another mistake?" I ask her. "Do you sometimes date men you know aren't right just because you're sure they won't break your heart?"

Giovanna sighs. "Look," she says. "All men are *stronzi.*"

Loosely translated, this means that all men are turds; but it isn't as harsh as it sounds in English. In Italian, *stronzi* can be sort of affectionate, like saying all men are dogs, but they can be good dogs.

I nod. I more or less agree.

"You just have to let men be men," she says. "They're different from women. Sometimes you Americans forget about that, you're so interested in having the man do the dishes, share his feelings, and pick out the perfect earrings for you. Sometimes it seems like you're looking for a man who will be your best girl friend. But you don't really want that. You want a man. You *want* a *stronzo*."

"You're right," I say. I mean, there's no way I'm doing all the dishes, but I do want a man who is a man. "A good stronzo."

"*Sì.*"

But the problem, I tell her, is that I can't tell one stronzo from another, a good dog from a bad dog, and I don't want to get bitten again.

"Relationships are sometimes wrong, but so you made a mistake, not a fatal error," Giovanna says, downing her espresso in one quick gulp. "You're smarter now."

I pick up the sliver of lemon rind on the espresso saucer and take a tiny bite. "In English, we have a term, an acronym, for bad relationships, bad experiences," I tell her. "AFOG. Another Fucking Opportunity for Growth." I tick the letters off on my fingers.

"*Afog,*" she pronounces in her Italian accent, and we both laugh.

We head back down the hill to the ferry, the light fading, Stromboli shooting sparks into the darkening sky, and make it back to our hotel. In the morning, after coffee, Giovanna leaves for Palermo, and I go to Naples, then back to Rome and home. We kiss cheeks, and she waves as I board the boat.

When I disembark in Naples, in the port area, I realize it's not the best part of town and I'm alone. I feel frozen for a second, things seem unfamiliar, and then I take a deep breath. I have been here before. I tuck in my jewelry, hold my passport and money close, and act as though I know where I'm going.

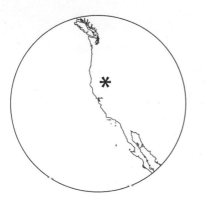

Chapter Eight

SAN FRANCISCO *
BUENOS AIRES

2005

It's February, and I'm celebrating my forty-fourth birthday, throwing a pizza party with my friend Guillermo, the Italians and Latin Americans competing against each other to see who can make the perfect crust, the guests happy for whatever combination of arugula, prosciutto, mozzarella, or mushrooms comes out of the kitchen next. I'm grateful for my lively group of friends, and many tell me, leaving the party, that they met so many interesting people.

Sandra helps me clean up, collecting wineglasses and washing dishes. "This was fun," she says, as we dry the last of the pile.

"Definitely," I say, flicking back the olive green boa my Italian friend Tonia gave me earlier in the evening. I pour us another glass of wine and we finally sit, sinking into the couch.

"Here's to a great year," she says, and we clink glasses. We revisit the guests—who was funny, who was the handsome guy with the gray hair, who didn't show up, when did so-and-so get divorced. "There were some really nice, interesting, smart men here," Sandra observes. "Why aren't you dating any of them?"

"There's a different, complicated reason for each one," I tell her. "Let's just say I'm lucky to have a lot of great friends."

"Things haven't exactly been easy for you in the past couple years, especially with men." She folds a dish towel. "I suppose it doesn't get easier for any of us after forty. It's tough terrain."

I nod. She's faced a lot of challenges herself: a child with learning difficulties, trying to keep her family afloat financially, having to move to the suburbs to find an affordable school. Almost anyone who is middle-aged can give you a long list of things that have gone wrong or that didn't turn out the way they expected. But at least by now we have some measure of experience and wisdom to deal with it all. "Things definitely aren't easy for anyone."

I have made progress, I tell her, in getting over my setback, a difficult experience that left me skittish with men, more aware of my vulnerability. I have even come to think that it's probably not such a bad thing that I am more in touch with that side of myself. But though I've dated a couple of men, even for a few months each, I still feel buffeted around by my fears. I'm also still unsure how to reconcile my wanderlust and desire for companionship and a home. In other words, I am right where I started when I headed out into my forties.

"Now I only have a year until I'm forty-five," I tell Sandra, "and that seems like the expiration date."

"For what?" Sandra asks.

"For finding a husband, a home, a family."

Sandra shakes her head. "We adopted Aldo when I was about your age," she says. "Your friend Ben adopted a kid when he was sixty. Nothing expires until you do."

*   *   *

STILL, AFTER SANDRA leaves and I go to bed—the mattress dips on my side, unbalanced—I decide I need to wage a campaign to find a real boyfriend before I turn forty-five. I'm not sure where to begin. The obvious place to start would be with the usual resolutions about losing weight, but I'm in good shape and by this age I realize that my problem with relationships is heavier than fifteen pounds, convenient as that excuse has been.

Actually, thinking about my weight reminds me that I did have a big success with a previous campaign, in my thirties, to learn to eat normally and feel better about my body. Having had a grim history of chaotic eating and hating my body, I decided, at thirty, to reinvent the way I eat. That involved going to Italy to learn to cook and eat like an Italian, with a good deal more discipline, sociability, and appreciation than I was theretofore accustomed to, always sitting down for meals instead of compulsively grazing by the light of the fridge. I managed to completely turn my eating around, learning how to respect and love food, becoming a good cook, even doing some stints as a food writer. I also developed a lot more appreciation for my healthy body, which is something I glimpsed only occasionally, in dance classes, in my twenties. That willful, positive change in my thirties—a serious personal accomplishment—is something I can hang on to now, to give me hope about this new campaign to improve myself, settle down, find a man, and somehow become a more balanced adult by forty-five.

But learning to eat properly and appreciate my curves was much more under my control than the prospect of finding a guy, which is kind of left up to the universe. Plus I'm still much more distrustful of men than I was before Samoa. And it's never been exactly easy to meet men in San Francisco. I'm particularly wary of dating online; there's no context for the person you're meeting in cyberspace, no longtime friend to assure you that he's a nice guy, not a psycho. The process is much more emotionally fraught and time-consuming than it would seem, just browsing a Man Catalogue, clicking on the witty architect who loves skiing and Italo Calvino, and having him delivered right to my door.

I already know from numerous attempts that I'm not very good at meeting strangers on blind dates. It's even worse than being in a small group and going around in a circle explaining what you want from the experience. You show up for a simple glass of wine, and for the next hour a guy evaluates all the ways in which you don't measure up to his ideal female. You walk in thinking that your various quirks and attributes—pug nose, edgy humor, smile lines, healthy ass—are all part of a package that makes you irresistibly lovable. You walk out, just one drink later, with a magnified awareness of your many defects. Eventually it all gets to be pretty defensive, not a great forum for showing what a giving, sweet woman you are. You arrive at the appointed time having not bothered to brush your hair, and right off your attitude is, You want to have a drink with me? Well, fuck you.

There has to be a better way to find a partner, but I have no idea what it is. I suspect it's not going to be a simple numbers game, a matter of sifting through enough online profiles. Somehow I think it's going to be more internal than external, that it'll take some kind of psychic shift. I burrow into my pillow and close my eyes; I have a year to figure it out.

A FEW WEEKS later, I drive over the Golden Gate Bridge into the headlands to go on a long hike with a dear friend, Kathy, who is a decade older than I am but who went to the same college and into the same profession and shares the same temperament and astrological sign. We are so much alike that we love each other fiercely as friends and at times get as strongly annoyed. She is not a traveler like I am, flying to different countries, but she is always off on another exploration into herself, whether through spiritual practices or a variety of self-help programs.

Independent, strong-willed, and softhearted, Kathy is in a long-term relationship but struggles because her boyfriend, though smart, doesn't have her intellectual thirst and sometimes just wants to drink beer and watch football with the boys and have that be okay. Conflicted, she stays, because she likes the coziness of their relationship, even if she refuses to get married and always has one foot partly out the door. She, too, is looking for balance between being a bright, strong, independent woman and making a relationship work.

While we're walking along a path between ferns and redwood trees, we talk about our relationships. We haven't seen each other in many months; I may have been avoiding her, because the last time we hiked, when I told her about Samoa, she reacted so strongly it made me feel as if I were permanently damaged, that I'd have to spend years in therapy to deal with the repercussions, when I just wanted to treat the episode like a bad case of food poisoning that I'd recovered from, except that I still shy away from eating scallops. Now that story is present but in the background.

I tell her I've dated a couple of people since then, cautiously, the most successful being Matthew, a psychologist I liked for his bright orange cashmere sweater and goofy smile, but wasn't attracted to right away. He is a gentleman, well traveled, well read, and funny, full of stories, so I relaxed and told him we should be friends. We went out every few weeks for dinner, having a great time, swapping travel tales, drinking French wine, until one evening he held my hand and it startled me so much I hailed a cab, jumped in, and barely waved good-bye. It wasn't until he took me to a Patti Smith concert—something akin to a spiritual experience for me—that we danced closely and then actually kissed.

For the next few months, I enjoyed being with someone eccentric and adventuresome; we drove down the coast to ride the roller coaster in Santa Cruz and then up to Napa to eat the season's best peaches. We sped through the curves up Mount Tamalpais at night in a convertible and walked barefoot on Stinson Beach. Then we decided on the spur of the moment to go together to Asia, where I had never been.

Matthew promised that the trip would involve cocktails at a resort by the beach in Thailand. He is such a great traveler, always off to Egypt, a beach village in Mexico, or some other remote, steaming place, that I told him to go ahead and make all the plans. I was frantically finishing up a big project and thought it would be an interesting experiment to have Matthew take care of everything, including me.

But when we landed in northernmost Malaysia, after a cramped and sweaty night on the Jungle Express from Singapore, one stop after all the locals keep motioning us to *get out* of the train, we found ourselves in a seriously Muslim neighborhood where Americans, particularly a guy with Howard Stern hair and a woman whose only head covering was a hoodie, were not particularly welcome. I no longer felt so protected. Our trip over the border by boat into southern Thailand had a similarly bad vibe, which got worse when we found a ride in the back of a pickup truck and the police stopped us, with great fanfare, to force one guy out, slap him around, and throw him into the back of their van. When we made it into town, it turned out that not only had Matthew, as eccentric and endearing as he is, not made reservations at a resort, it was hurricane season. Muslims and monsoons: no cocktails on the beach.

We spent a couple of days wandering around Narathiwat, with no other tourists in sight, me huddled under my hoodie. There was a time when I might have found that kind of travel exhilarating, but on that trip I felt fearful and exposed. We made the best of the situation, sampling exceptional street food, visiting a giant golden Buddha, but the atmosphere was vaguely menacing and I was happy to return to Singapore. As cities go, Singapore has amazing street food, a colorful Indian section, and some nice orchids, but otherwise it resembles a giant mall from which you cannot escape.

Our romance did not survive the long flight back to San Francisco, and we took separate taxis home. Three weeks later, when I read about extremists burning secular schools in Narathiwat and people killed, I e-mailed Matthew to tell him what danger we'd been in. "So what?" he e-mailed back. "The Twin Towers were safe on September 10th."

Kathy stops midhike, turns around in the trail, and crosses her arms. "Laura," she says, "you need someone who can take better care of you. Especially after what happened. There's no shame in wanting to feel protected; we all need that."

"I know," I tell Kathy. I'm not sure I should tell her about my other short-term relationship. "I actually did date someone else who wanted to take care of me, but it was kind of the wrong way."

Since this is a ten-mile hike, I launch into the story about the artist I met on a trip back from Switzerland, in the Frankfurt airport, browsing in the duty-free shop. The scruffy short man in a photographer's vest chatted with me, and since he had a seven-hour layover, I invited him into the airport lounge as my guest. We had a pleasant talk for twenty minutes before I had to leave, him mostly saying something unintelligible about physics that somehow related to his art, and we exchanged e-mail addresses on the back of napkins.

When I get home I Googled him and realized that though I didn't particularly care for his art, all surface and no soul, he was rather famous and quite wealthy, for an artist. He flew to San Francisco to take me to lunch at one of my favorite places, where we ate two dozen oysters with a delicious bottle of wine. He marveled at how down to earth I was when I told him I could hop a bus home—no one he knows takes the bus. He was fascinating, with a huge imagination, telling me about his projects all over the world.

I heard from him several times, calling me with updates from Japan or Greece or an island in the Pacific. Then he sent me first-class tickets to see an opening of his show in Bilbao, and of course I went, staying in a luxury hotel right by the Guggenheim Museum, enchanted by the city's art and architecture, finding a wonderful place to eat squid in its own ink, chatting in Spanish with young strangers at the packed opening. After the opening, I ran into the artist having dinner with some donors or gallery people. I congratulated him, and he acted as if I were a stranger, shaking my hand, not bothering to introduce me to the people he was seated with.

"Please tell me you didn't see him again," says Kathy.

"I did." We met up a few days later in Sardinia, staying at a four-star inn tucked up against granite cliffs near Nuoro, in the middle of the island, going to the ocean to explore its coves by boat, visiting villages, watching a parade of local costumes.

On our last evening, the artist told me he was in love with me and wanted to buy me a house in Ojai to live in so that I could always be there when he returned from his trips. But I don't know anybody in Ojai. I realized it would be easy to stay with this guy and be wealthy for the rest of my years. I could get used to the $600 bottles of wine he orders at dinner, especially if every sip didn't remind me I was drinking up half my rent. I could fly with him to one of his islands when he wanted me to come along, or to the Biennale in Venice or the Hermitage in Saint Petersburg when he had a show. I could travel whenever I desired, not worry about having to make a living, and have time to write what I please. It was tempting.

Even Kathy, I can tell, suspiciously quiet on the trail, is tempted.

At home, I heard from the artist, when he was in airports or checking into hotels. We saw each other a few times when he passed through San Francisco. Often, he would say he was coming and then forget or cancel. He'd apologize but say that's just the way he is, he does that to senators and wealthy art collectors, too, and then he'd tell me again how we were meant to be together.

Kathy groans.

"I know, he can't be trusted, not even to show up," I say. "When he left me waiting at one of San Francisco's best restaurants, me pretending I had planned all along to enjoy a five-course tasting menu by myself on Valentine's Day, I finally called and said that's not how my friends treat me, it's a matter of the most basic respect, and being rich and famous doesn't make up for bad manners and he could go fuck himself."

"It took you long enough," Kathy says.

"I was never serious about him," I said. "The truth is that I really didn't like his art, so that was a deal breaker."

"That and the fact that he had no respect for you."

"Yeah."

We walk along quietly for a while. Clearly, I tell Kathy, I haven't figured out how to find a man who can take care of me, and vice versa. It is a mystery to me how other women attract men who wait in the car when they drop them off to see that they're safely in the house, pay for meals, get up in the middle of the night to bring them a glass of water, and inquire solicitously after their needs. I find guys who want to be buddies, split the check, and figure I can make it home fine by myself.

I always appreciate Kathy's advice, because she's so sensitive and smart, but I never know quite where it will come from. Each time I see her, she's passionate about some new diet, spiritual practice, twelve-step program, exercise regimen, or Eastern philosophy. Now she tells me she's into *The Rules,* the popular book of retro advice on how to get a man to love you, it seems to me, by being aloof, falsely helpless, and manipulative. This shocks me, because Kathy is usually more likely to extol the virtues of Merleau-Ponty or Thich Nhat Hanh.

"I know, I know, it doesn't seem feminist," Kathy tells me. "But if you think about it, it really is. It's about getting respect from men. Make them work to get you. It's your job to be as pretty and interesting as you can be, then sit back and let them respond to you."

"Ick," I say, even though I'm trying to listen to her and not just be automatically appalled. "It's too much of a game." I am not, for instance, wearing mascara here on the trail just in case we run into the man of my dreams. Nor, if some man contacts me, am I going to wait until he badgers me three more times before I respond; that doesn't seem friendly or polite, not to mention real. "If you can't be your real self with someone, what's the point?"

"Why is it being your authentic self to run after men, to send them e-mails first, pay for dinner, and not let yourself be taken care of once in a while?" asks Kathy. "Men are hunters, they want to go after you." I cringe thinking about buying dinners for Gustavo when he was broke, telling him I was on an expense account, which is probably not something you should do with a Latin male. I suppose I was trying too hard. Still.

"I don't like feeling like prey," I say. All those years of female liberation, uneasy as they may have been, and we're back to this. "Nor do I want to go into a hut once a month when I have my period or get thrown onto a funeral pyre with my dead husband."

"It's not about giving up power, it's about keeping your power," Kathy says. "You're always telling me about jumping into bed with men and then feeling disappointed that it doesn't work out. You want men who respect you."

I'm regretting telling her about a couple of those episodes. "Respect, sure," I say. "But the rest is phony. I'm not some passive-aggressive creature trying to trick a man into marrying her. I want a funny, intelligent guy who likes me, who has chemistry with me, and who is, you know, different but equal. I'm a confident grown-up woman."

"Sure," says Kathy. "Real confidence is sexy to men. But there's a difference between being confident with men and being aggressive, which isn't sexy. There's also a difference between being receptive and being passive."

"So what's the difference?"

"Fear."

"And so how can you manage not to be afraid, especially with that whole hunter-and-prey dynamic?"

"Real strength comes from being able to show your vulnerability but hold on to yourself. You can attract men by being receptive but say no to them until you get to know them and trust them."

"Maybe, but you can't do that by following some ridiculous 'Rules.' " And I don't want to trap everyone I sleep with into a relationship. "This isn't the 1950s." You just have to understand the reality of the situation so you don't feel disappointed. I mean, that one takes a little work sometimes (i.e., Gustavo)—but still.

"Okay," says Kathy, sighing. "Forget the 'Rules.' Think of it instead as ballroom dancing." Now she has my attention. "In order to dance, you have to be able to follow, to be receptive to a man's touch. To do that, you need to hold yourself in your own space, not be draped all over him, and give him pressure back when he pushes you. You have to be strong and confident enough in your own body to be receptive to his."

"That makes more sense."

We stop talking as we hike through the trees to a big vista of the Pacific Ocean. Sometimes, when I'm hiking around Marin, I wonder why I need to travel so far away to be awed.

WHEN I GET home, put on some music, and run a bath, I consider our conversation. There is no doubt that whatever I've been doing, with regard to men, hasn't been working. I keep thinking it has to do with luck, with running into the right man, but perhaps there's more to it than that. There is a certain amount of fear, after my marriage and my experience in Samoa, which I try to cover up by being tough, clever, reserved. But what Kathy said about being more receptive to men while holding on to your power and your own space made some sense. Being receptive is a good practice for anyone, male or female.

But I'm not going to practice by dating online. That chapter is over. I swish around in the bubbles and decide I need to try a completely different approach. I somehow need a forum where I can learn about receptivity on a deep level, without the fear of rejection and hurt that always accompanies dating, someplace completely safe. I need to practice being approachable and responsive, like being led in a dance.

I lie there soaking, listening to the music, a group called the Gotan Project, some modern tangoish music, and then drain the tub. I jump up and grab a towel. I am going to learn to tango.

THE IDEA BEHIND taking tango classes isn't quite as straightforward as hoping I will run into the man of my dreams at a *milonga,* though that could certainly happen; I love a man who can dance. I'm thinking of it as part of my self-improvement effort, which might help me develop the right kind of energy to attract the right man—hopefully, by the time I turn forty-five.

Tango, for the woman—or for the follower, anyway, because in San Francisco, of course, men can be followers and women leaders—is all about playing the traditional woman's role: passive, responsive, flirtatious, tempting but even more erotic in its restraint. It's fun and full of frisson. Maybe a little tango could teach me something about letting go of control, allowing myself to be led. As ridiculous as it seems to try to realign the basic way you relate to men in your forties, I figure a little tango couldn't hurt.

So I buy some sturdy jazz heels and a flippy black skirt and sign up for classes.

From the first session, I realize it's not going to be easy. For one thing, it's obvious that I am not built like most women tango dancers, who tend to be delicate and lean, wear slinky dresses slit up to the thigh, and have disproportionately long legs. My physique is better suited for African, Brazilian, or salsa dance, by which I mean I was born with a rather steatopygic derriere and sturdy, muscular legs. (When I was dancing at a party in Kenya once, a local gentleman remarked, "You are very unusual for a white woman," which I took as a compliment, and, were I not planning to be cremated, I might have etched on my tombstone.) Since tango is all in the leaning torso, flicking legs, and coquettish footwork—not in the grooving hips—I do the best I can.

I'm a pretty good dancer. I've taken hundreds of dance classes over the years, but almost always dancing solo in groups. I get jittery dancing with a partner. It makes me feel like I did in third grade, at a piano recital, suddenly so self-conscious I blanked on the music. It's as if when someone is holding my arms I can no longer feel the rhythm in my feet. At tango class, I learn the steps, but my constant challenge is to trust my partner to hold my weight and to wait for him to move, not to anticipate or lead. At one point a partner steps back, crosses his arms, and, when I finally notice him, asks me when I am going to stop twirling around by myself. They're difficult lessons.

But I keep going to class and then to milongas and realize that you can dance tango every night of the week in San Francisco if you like, and a lot of obsessed people do. I sit there and wait, as if at a high school dance, for a man across the room to nod to me, so I can nod back, and he drifts over and offers me his hand. Often it is a little too much like a high school dance, where I just sit there, pretending to find something fascinating at the bottom of my drink. But sometimes I spin around the floor and, for a few minutes, feel light and sexy, my body responding to whatever move the man desires.

T HE   TANGO   LESSONS seem to work a little magic when I have my first date with Evan, a college friend of a friend I meet at a dinner party. I let him decide where to eat, even though, in picking restaurants and ordering dishes, I'm usually what my friend Anne calls a "restaurant top." Instead, I try what he suggests—the Korean barbecue is wonderful—listen to him and respond, and squelch the impulse to take over the conversation, to tell stories and entertain him, which is what I always do when I'm uncomfortable. He takes me to his favorite bar in Oakland, Cafe Van Cleef, which is my favorite bar in that town, too. It's the kind of place where, after a couple of drinks, you can show someone how to hold you in a tango embrace and no one glances your way. His goatee tickles me. "I like that," he says, his hand lingering on my waist. "We should go dancing sometime."

But I am actually leaving in a couple days to go to Buenos Aires to study tango and its feminine wiles more seriously. That news seems to lend some urgency to our date. On the way back to the car, Evan pulls me into an alcove on a deserted downtown street and kisses me.

"You're so pretty," he tells me. "Do people always tell you that?"

"Not *always*," I say with a little smile. Like maybe not since the Reagan administration.

We go back to his house and play on his couch for a while, but when he wants to have sex—"Why not, do you think we're going to get married or something?" is a revealing comment—I have the good tangoish sense to insist on going home after a little more kissing and general appreciation of my body. "Here's to full-bodied people," he says, as if we are just that much more full of life. I move to get up from the couch, and he holds me down with his beefy arms, looking me straight in the eyes with his bright blues. I have a leap of feeling and for a moment think it's fear or panic. Then I close my eyes and breathe; I remember this feeling, it's not fear, it's excitement; it's feeling hot.

"Open your eyes," he says. "I want you to think about this in Buenos Aires. This is exactly how I'm going to fuck you when you get home."

That leaves quite an impression on me, but I have a plane ticket and am on a mission. Never mind that I seem to have a habit of meeting promising men and then leaving on a trip; I am on a campaign to learn how to be better in a relationship. Plus I've landed an assignment writing about being a *turista tanguera* in Buenos Aires, so it's a work gig.

WHEN I STEP out of the taxi in Buenos Aires, I am infatuated. The town is a faded beauty, with elegant, decaying European architecture wearily trying to ignore the brash new concrete neighbors. Intellectual, poetic Argentines have weathered unspeakable political and economic tragedy, which partly explains why there are more psychologists per capita than in Manhattan. Buenos Aires is sexy and the one place where I can speak my combination of Italian and Spanish and everyone will understand me. It could even be a perfect place to find a man who has read Jorge Luis Borges and Julio Cortázar, backward and forward, has a nice cellar full of Malbec, and can sweep me off my feet dancing tango.

I stay at the Tango Academy in San Telmo, the neighborhood where the dance was born—in its brothels, as a kind of foreplay, before it became more respectable and stylized—and still thrives in late-night corner bars. I want to take lessons and slide right into the scene. The hotel proprietors make me feel at home amid the worn velvet drapes, spiral staircases, wrought-iron balconies, and high chandeliers, and I love the cheap glamour of the place.

The first evening, I go to a tango lesson at the hotel, where I meet other turistas tangueras (many of them American couples whose wives aren't thrilled to have their husbands trading partners) and locals who are willing to twirl a beginner around the floor. Anders, a handsome Swede, though too young for me (barely drinking age), is a perfect partner, leading me assuredly across the dance floor. I also meet Claudia, a forty-two-year-old Mexican film location scout, who drifts with me from tango practice to late-night milongas, stopping to drink a glass of cheap Bonarda wine and eat succulent grass-fed steaks when our feet are too sore to dance.

Claudia has thick dark hair and big eyes; she's attractive and accomplished in a creative field. Like me, she is divorced with no children and wondering what's happening next. She also loves to travel and is considering a move to Argentina. She is fed up with Mexico City because there are no men there, the way I am fed up with San Francisco, the way urban women in their early forties are fed up with cities in the entire postindustrialized world. She seeks solace in tango, when she can drift in a man's arms and feel him leading her and then move on to the next encounter. Her relationships are like that, too; last night she met a gorgeous man in his early thirties, said good-bye to him before coffee, and now rolls her eyes at his text message on her cell, though she'll probably meet up with him again later on. Claudia has stopped having any expectations of men except to dance with them, and sleep with them when it's convenient and fun. She seems pretty happy with this arrangement; it's one that has made me happy, too, at times, just not necessarily the next morning. She's focusing on her career and her move and isn't worried about having a partner, though her family in Mexico thinks she's crazy, an old maid, ruining her last chances.

We go daily to the Confitería Ideal, a grand old ballroom with tarnished mirrors, worn tablecloths, and white-jacketed waiters, for afternoon milongas. We wait on the sideline with the other women, nervously sipping water, for men to ask us to dance with a glance from across the room. The *porteños*—B.A. natives—are friendly, and the dapper, aging men give me courtly advice as we dance, calling me "bambina," or "little girl." I dance with perhaps fifty men at the classes, each two-minute dance like a one-night stand—physically close but emotionally distant. Only such strict indifference allows people to rub their chests close and intertwine their legs, moving across the floor like caressing skin.

Since Claudia and I both speak Italian, we are in demand by a couple of gentlemen visiting from Florence. Otherwise, aside from the classes, I sit out a lot of dances. Tango is a real meritocracy: men choose women not for their beauty or youth but for their ability to close their eyes and meld into the man's lead. The woman who gets the most dances, bless her, is a short, stout señora in her seventies with a sparkling blouse and a skirt slit to the knee.

Discouraged on the dance floor, I try to find a regular partner, someone I can relax with and work on a few steps. I go on Match.com, saying I am seeking a man who can show me the tango scene for an article. Many men contact me—being a relatively blond American seems to hold a certain allure in B.A.—sending me virtual *besos,* but most want quick *sexo.* I chat with a couple by phone but violate some cultural rule by brazenly suggesting coffee; men, it seems, do all the inviting in Argentina. It's a tango thing. One man wants to take me to an Argentine ranch but won't meet me for coffee first, and I am not about to set out for the distant pampas alone with him.

Then Juan Miguel, a fifty-year-old, cueball-pated architect who also teaches yoga, contacts me. He invites me out to a trendy Middle Eastern restaurant in Palermo Viejo, reaches for my hand over dessert, and makes poetic comments about my appearance. "*Piel como terciopelo.*" Skin like velvet. "*Ojos como topacio.*" Eyes like topaz. He correctly guesses my astrological sign—"You're such a free-spirited woman, you must be Aquarius"—which makes him think we might be fated for each other.

But it is not to be. After dinner, we go to a crowded milonga, where Juan Miguel drives me around the dance floor like a bumper car, crashing into other couples, whose female partners adroitly jab me with their spiked heels. No one, including Juan Miguel, has a sense of humor about things. In fact, tango and Argentina in general seem to lack a spirit of fun. *No más.*

Back home in San Francisco, the tango scene is less inviting than in B.A. In Argentina, the men understand that the point of dancing with a woman is to make her look beautiful, to dance well together, so they lead at your level. With a strong leader who has nothing to prove, even if all you can do is a basic step and a few forward *ochos,* you look and feel graceful, transcending the steps and sliding into a subtle sense of rhythm, connection, and, for small, restrained moments, passion. Not so in San Francisco, where men tend to learn complicated routines in classes and force you to stumble through them without establishing a basic connection, then slowly leading you to something a little trickier. There's also an atmosphere of formality and strictness at the milongas and an emphasis on technique that isn't quite suited to my personality.

As much as I love the elegance and glamour of tango, as well as the tragic romance of the music, I start leaving my tango shoes in the back of the closet. I've learned something about letting go of control, holding on to my space, and making myself receptive to a man's lead, but I've also learned that tango really isn't my dance. For me, dancing is an expression of joy, music entering your body like spirits, releasing them through movement. Tango is too restrained for me and not enough fun; any dance where you aren't supposed to shake your ass is clearly made for someone else's body.

Instead, I think, I'll sign up for salsa lessons.

*   *   *

AT HOME, EVAN calls to invite me to a baseball game. I walk
to the ballpark under a clear San Francisco sky, watching people
happily making their way from downtown offices to the stadium
by the bay. Evan meets me with Mardi Gras beads in the Giants'
colors to wear and takes my hand to lead me to the bleachers.
I love the crowd's good-hearted cheering, stomping, and booing
and the friendly way everyone in the bleachers chats with one another. I spread out a little tablecloth on the bleachers and surprise
Evan with a picnic: Australian wine, Italian prosciutto, pecorino,
and olives. He turns from the ball game, takes a few bites, and
groans with home-run enthusiasm. "I love you," he says, which I
take to mean "I love this picnic," and he kisses me on the lips.

Later, walking toward the Muni bus, the Bay Bridge glit-
tering in the background, Evan puts his arms around my soft,
custom-made Argentine leather jacket. "I would love to go traveling with you," he says. "Where in the whole world would you
like to go?"

I put my hands in his pockets. Nepal? The Seychelles? Back
to those Sicilian islands? I rest my head on his shoulder, still jet-
lagged, and he strokes my hair.

"How about dinner at my house?" I say, and he gives me another kiss.

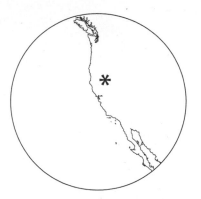

I decide to stay at home for a while to see how things develop in my personal life, if given a chance. I sort through my closet as a vicarious way of rummaging through my personal issues, creating some order in my life. I feel the need to toss out old stuff, pare down to things that are really important to me, let go of things I've been hanging on to, like jeans I bought ten years ago, hoping I'd lose fifteen pounds. Maybe I should figure out how to do this process internally, but for now I'm just cleaning my closet.

I come across my old wedding dress, a simple, tea-length chiffony frock that doesn't scream "bride"; I wore it to my friend Cecilia's fiftieth birthday party at a winery with a big garden hat and flip-flops and no one had the slightest clue about its former, now-tattered glory. Eyeing my pile of clothes to give away, I have to acknowledge that floaty, off-white dresses in general have limited use but am reluctant to part with it. In the spirit of renewal, I have the bright idea of dyeing my old wedding dress to wear to a party. This strikes me as a good idea, like when I swapped the stones in my wedding ring, added a few more bands to symbolize more happy relationships in my life, and shifted them to my right hand as divorce rings.

So I run to the fabric store, pick out the first color that catches my eye, ignore the directions, and throw the dye in the wash with the dress. When it comes out a splotchy Halloween orange instead of the pretty coral on the box, I cry—for my ruined dress, my stupidity, and my relationships that have failed partly due to my darned impatience. I wished I could start over: undye the dress, take back what I said, and look before I leaped.

I guess I've always had mild issues with what psychologists call impulse control. I know I'm not the person to rely upon to say "no" to things, whether it's another glass of wine, late-night dancing at a dive club, or a five-day trip into the Sinai Desert with Bedouins I just met a few hours ago. I rarely stop to weigh pros and cons, risks and benefits, long-term costs, and, worst of all, more sensitive people's reactions. I like to do things fast, and do them now. It's hard for me to resist my urges—to buy cobalt blue shoes, book a trip to Italy, or tell someone off. This does me no good: If I'm upset with a friend or colleague, I'll whip off a scathing e-mail. I jump into flirtations with men I barely know and then get furiously hurt when they aren't in love with me. I always say what's on my mind, even when my mind isn't fully engaged. My actions are immediate, but the consequences—embarrassment, burned bridges, badly fitting boots—are lasting. Basically, I could use a pause button.

Not long after I leave my former wedding dress in a free box on the sidewalk in the Haight for a homeless person to wear, a magazine editor calls to ask what my worst trait is. "Impulsiveness," I immediately reply. When she then suggests I go see a woman named Sharon Salzberg for some help and then write about it, I instantly agree. It isn't until I'm on the plane, reading the blurb on one of her books, *Lovingkindness,* that I discover that Salzberg is one of the country's leading meditation teachers. I've done it again! By not thinking things through, I've landed in a disastrous situation. The last thing I am capable of doing is sitting still to meditate. I'll do it wrong, fail to write the story, and, the way things are going, end up waiting tables. I am an idiot, but there's no turning back.

I arrive at the hotel where Sharon is staying, expecting to meet an ethereal, remote woman in flowing robes and maybe a shaved head. But when she opens the door to her room, she is casual, sharp, and funny—with a New York accent—and somehow makes me feel as if I've known her for years.

I dive right in, explaining that I suspect I act rashly because I can't bear to sit with uncomfortable feelings. I'm always booking plane tickets to run away from them, I say. In the past, I managed my emotions by the mouthful, using food to stuff down pangs of loneliness, rejection, unworthiness, or failure. When I was younger, the fact that I had such little impulse control led to some seriously chaotic eating problems, which I eventually overcame. But even after I learned to eat more mindfully, savoring every taste and smell, my impulsiveness just spun out in new directions: shooting off my mouth, cutting my own bangs, getting overly invested and upset about a guy whose profile I first read on Match.com the morning before, and making a general mess of my life.

Sharon seems both amused and sympathetic and observes

that my impulsiveness isn't all bad—it's a quality that's related to being spontaneous, vivid, and generous. It's true: I'm happy to throw a spur-of-the-moment dinner party, I'm quick with a retort, and I never have to return to a boutique to discover that the dress I wanted is gone. I even have a few friends left. Sharon tells me I shouldn't be so hard on myself for my impulsiveness but learn to make my temperament work for my benefit. "You can prize that adventurous spirit and become more mindful of times when you're hurting yourself or others," she says. What I need is to slow down my speed and momentum, take time to investigate my feelings, and create a private sense of pause. Then my reactions would be a choice, not a compulsion.

Fine, but can she fix me? Now?

Sharon suggests that I begin, as I did with my eating problems, by tuning in to pure sensation. The pace of our lives is so fast, she says, that we scarcely notice what's going on around us. We get so caught up in achieving our desires and avoiding our discomforts; we're preoccupied with plans, distracted with wondering what other people think about us. But something as simple as concentrating on the cool, soothing sensations of washing my hands, the taste and smell of hot tea, or the rhythm of my breath could bring me back to an awareness of the present.

That all sounds lovely, *but I am impatient.* "What I need," I say, "is an emergency pause button."

Sharon smiles and contemplates that. First, she suggests, I could get into the habit of saving my e-mails as drafts before hitting "Send." Just that, I agree, could have prevented some serious professional and romantic embarrassment. And when a strong emotion bubbles up, I could stop to check in with my physical sensations: is my stomach clenched, heart pumping, brow sweating? That inventory might delay me long enough not to swear at a traffic cop or hang up on my sister. Given a few moments and deep breaths, I might see that those physical sensations subside and realize that anger, fear, and disappointment aren't as solid and immovable as they seem. Fierce emotions don't always have to be shoved away; they can be like a storm that passes.

I like the idea of being still in a tempest, not always buffeted about, feeling compelled to react. Now that I have a couple of tools for emergencies, maybe I could leave. But Sharon makes it clear that developing a habit of tuning in to myself, of being mindful, is going to take some practice. That practice, she says, is called meditation.

That's when I'm ready to bolt. The one time I tried meditating, my mind didn't go blank; it wandered off wildly. Plus I'd done everything wrong. I was at a Zen center and accidentally put my feet where people eat and bowed the wrong way, and bald, black-cloaked monks yelled at me in fervent whispers. Sharon assured me that the "insight" or "Vipassana" meditation she practices isn't as formal as Zen—pretty schlumpy, really, by comparison—which appeals to me. Nor am I doing everything wrong if I don't achieve a blank mental canvas or state of bliss right away. The point of meditating, she says, isn't to empty your thoughts but to develop an awareness of them, watch them with an almost clinical eye. You concentrate on one object, such as your breath, but you're not messing up if you get distracted. That's just an opportunity to notice where your mind has strayed and gently start over. The practice of letting go—of obsessions, plans, feelings, attachments—and starting over again with compassion for yourself eventually affects the way you live.

"When you've blurted out a comment, you don't lose heart and get discouraged," Sharon says. "You just start over." Hopefully, you reach a point where you don't make unwise comments to begin with.

Now it's time to try it out. I am anxious, but Sharon tells me to just close my eyes and get comfortable in my chair. She leads me in three exercises that turn out to be surprisingly simple, with no secret mantras or chanting. One is a sitting meditation, watching my breathing, feeling it rise in my chest or stomach, and practicing letting go of whatever thoughts intrude without judging them, bringing my attention back to my breath. The exercise is like herding stray cats out of my brain; every time I chase one away, another is right there, yowling for attention. Then there is a walking meditation, where we slowly pace around her hotel room as if through peanut butter, focusing on subtle physical sensations, hopefully to the exclusion of nagging, neurotic thoughts.

Finally, she leads me through a "lovingkindness" meditation, where I am to silently offer good wishes to myself and others: "May you be safe, May you be happy, May you be healthy, May you live in ease." In this meditation, she instructs me to begin by offering kindness to myself, then to my dearest family and friends, and then work my way through neutral people I've encountered but don't feel one way or another about, then on to annoying people, and then eventually, with practice, to really difficult people, such as my ex-husband and Dick Cheney (I don't make it that

far). This meditation is supposed to develop a wellspring of compassion for myself and other people I deal with. "It's like giving
yourself a gift," Sharon tells me.

After I try these meditations with Sharon, I have to admit I
feel calm and refreshed, a state that lasts even through the lines
and delays at the airport. Once home, I take her advice to meditate every day for fifteen minutes. It is a lot harder without her
leading me through, like trying to do yoga by yourself at home.
During the first few sessions, I am angry that my timer is broken
(it isn't; it just seems as though time has stopped). My back hurts,
my legs fall asleep, my nose itches, and my brain goes racing all
over the place. I feel bursts of sadness, hilarity, recrimination, and
despair. But I do sit it out. Occasionally I reach a space where I
feel as if I am wearing internal noise-canceling headphones. During one session, I have a clear image of my mind as a cluttered
attic, furnished with all sorts of old petty grievances, grudges,
and fears. I am starting to clear away some of the debris, giving
myself room to move and breathe. And at night I begin having
dreams where instead of flipping out for getting a parking ticket
or having my credit card rejected, I let my anger go. Clearly,
something is going on in my unconscious that my waking mind
doesn't yet grasp.

Eventually, I notice a few times when my mind presses the
pause button on its own. When I lose my purse, I check the car
before panicking. I pass an adorable pair of emerald green sandals and hear a little voice say, "I have enough shoes." Waiting
in line with an inept clerk, I don't have cartoon flames shooting
from my head, I just suppose the poor guy is having a trying day.

Distressed about a situation with an article I'm working on, in-stead of snapping at the fact checker, I ask if I can call her back later. When I e-mail Evan and he doesn't respond, I don't im-mediately think, "That close-minded asshole probably thinks I'm too fat or too old, so fuck him"; instead I think, well, maybe he's got something else going on, I just don't know and we'll see.

After a month, I am so excited by my newfound patience that when I get an e-mail announcing a ten-day silent meditation re-treat, I don't pause, I sign right up.

As soon as I arrive at the Spirit Rock meditation center in Marin County, epicenter of the New Age, I realize that once again, I've made a mess. I've failed to think things through, I've made a ridiculous decision, and now I am being punished for my impulsiveness. The retreat center is pretty enough, with hik-ing trails in the hills and a lovely meditation hall, but the place is full of aliens, people who affect Asian robes, beam goodness, and shuffle around looking at their feet. Meditation may help me become a more patient person and increase my chances of find-ing a partner by forty-five, but I'm definitely not going to find a guy to fall in love with at a Vipassana retreat, especially since I won't have a chance to even speak to anyone. I'm supposed to stay here—completely silent!—for ten days.

The first day isn't so bad. They assign each of us a chore— mine is cleaning the kitchen floors, which involves slopping a satisfyingly loud amount of water around in the quiet atmo-sphere—and we meditate for several sessions, followed by a dharma talk by one of the retreat leaders, who surprises me with his dry and delightful sense of humor. At the end of that day I feel virtuous and refreshed—and quite ready to go home.

That night, sharing a cell-like dorm room with a frizzy-haired woman in Guatemalan pants, I resent the slurpy tooth-brushing and grooming noises she makes and the rude and selfish way she keeps her light on until late. Then comes the second day. The first forty-five-minute "sit" is grueling, starting well before daylight and caffeine (which isn't recommended, but I have some anyway). After breakfast, where everyone moves too slowly through the buffet line and makes annoying chewing sounds, I go to a succession of forty-five-minute sits, with breaks in between, as if I am attending classes at a school where absolutely nothing happens. Each session is an eternity long, people breathe and sniff too loudly all around me, noisily shifting their cushions and props, and all I can think about, aside from lunch, all the work I have to do when I got back, the pain in my right hip, and how many frequent-flier miles I need to amass before I regain my executive status, is when the hell is the bell going to ring? Between sits, I pick up a novel and read, parched for words and entertainment.

By afternoon I am going nuts with boredom and can fixate only on the fact that I am just a few minutes away from Point Reyes Station, where I know a restaurant that serves Sierra Nevada Pale Ale on tap. I don't think anyone has ever meditated so long on a cold pint of Sierra Nevada Pale Ale—its slightly bitter taste and golden color, its perfection among beers, how supremely thirst-relieving it would be in the midst of a hot Marin County summer afternoon, how well it would go with a medium-rare

Nieman Ranch hamburger with bleu cheese instead of all this
vegetarian hippie food, how my body would feel bathed in it to
my chin. Breathe in pale ale, breathe out pale ale. May I be safe,
may I be happy, may I be healthy, may I drink pale ale. May all
beings everywhere drink pale ale.

The second day, we have a small-group meeting with one
of the retreat leaders, and I am assigned to Sharon. I was hoping
the fact that it is a silent retreat would mean that we wouldn't
have to go around the circle and share how the retreat is going
for us, but this seems to be the one exception to the no-talking
rule. As usual, I instantly have the feeling I have in small groups
where you have to go around and introduce yourself and talk
about your feelings, of a mood ring that has turned black, a mis-
anthropist who wants nothing more than to be anywhere but in
a small group going around the circle. One by one, the participants describe how calm the retreat is making them feel, what
a wonderful opportunity it is for them to deal with their pain,
grief, anxiety, and impatience and search for meaning; how already they can feel themselves opening up and accepting, achieving a sense of balance, purpose, and equanimity. Only a couple
people admit to any problems; they are basically confused about
whether they should focus on breathing into their nostrils or their
stomachs when they meditate and relax visibly when Sharon tells
them there is no one right way.

Then it is my turn. I give a calm smile, as if to show that I, too,
am reveling in a higher state, off swimming with the dolphins in
my own personal pool of serotonin. Then I open my mouth. "All
I want," I blurt, "is to get into my car, drive to Point Reyes, and
have a nice cold pint of Sierra Nevada Pale Ale." Then I glance

around the room, looking surprised and slightly offended, as if that outburst had come from someone else.

There is silence. Unlike at the rest of the retreat, this is silence you can hear, loud silence. I don't believe everyone is stunned into realizing how much they, too, desire a pale ale; they are doing their karmic best not to be judgmental about what an unenlightened, impulsive, alcohol-addled bitch they have in their presence. And then Sharon gives a gentle laugh, a kind laugh, a real laugh, not laughing at me, exactly, but at how funny people are in general, working themselves up so about being in a small group and bursting out with the truth about wanting a beer.

"If you'd like to go get a beer, Laura, then why don't you?" Sharon says. This is an honest offer, not a leave-and-don't-ever-come-back threat. People in the group sigh, perhaps relieved, perhaps disappointed I'm not getting thrown off the island, as in *Survivor*. "No one says you can't take a little break if you need it," she continues in her sensible voice. "This is your first time, you're here for you, do what you need to do. Sometimes it helps to take time out during the first few days."

Well, that deflates my angst. That's like someone telling me, when I'm on a diet, that dark molten chocolate cake has no calories; it suddenly makes no difference whether I eat it all right away or not. Once I give myself permission to go have a beer, it loses its urgent appeal. I am no longer defying an authority I presumed was there, going against the rules just because I hate rules in general. I have a free choice. So I decide it is getting kind of late for a beer if I want to get back in time for the dharma talk this evening, and I can go tomorrow instead.

I don't leave the next day or the rest of the ten days, which go by surprisingly fast. Instead of hating being silent for all that time, which all of my friends thought would be impossible for such a chatty raconteuse, I feel profoundly relieved that for the first time since I was a toddler I don't have to speak. If I said anything to anyone I'd feel I had to entertain them, tell them a story, give them a favorable impression of myself, put them at ease, flirt, tell them where I live and what I do for a living, and then have to explain that yes, sometimes you come up with story ideas yourself and sometimes the magazine calls you, and no, generally you do not submit the same story to a lot of different magazines at once. I am free to be anonymous and observe, like being in a foreign country where you don't speak the language. You're just there, your most simple, reliable self.

I get into a rhythm with meditating. I don't go to all the sessions, respecting my limits and restlessness; I ditch one session a day to do yoga, which I figure is almost as good as meditating, and another to hike on the trails, which is perhaps better. On one of those walks, I encounter a rattlesnake, notice his lovely pattern, say, "Hello there, feller," to his flicking face, and keep on walking while he slithers into the grass. That's when I know all this meditation is having a seriously calming effect. Ordinarily, I'd have to be loaded on benzodiazepines to see a rattlesnake without screaming, having heart palpitations, and bursting into a sour sweat.

The last rattlesnake I ran into, for instance, was quite a different story. It was dusk on the day my ex-husband proposed to me, and we were taking a walk in the La Sal Mountains above Moab. My new fiancé asked me if I had any fears; every time in our relationship when we'd come clean with our fears, we'd ended up feeling closer. He said he was afraid that since he'd been abandoned as a kid, he might do the same thing to me or even abandon his own child if we had one, which we were planning to do. I reassured him that his fears were normal and unfounded. Abandon me? I could never imagine him doing that. Then he asked me about my fears, and I told him I didn't have any. Just at that moment I heard a distinctive, dry rattle. There, two feet from my left foot, thick as a fire hose, a rattlesnake was coiled up, warning to strike. I screamed and ran. When he caught up with me, my fiancé, who knew I was terrified of snakes, instead of comforting me, admonished me that I shouldn't have jumped, it was stupid, because snakes will jump right after you. I later thought of that snake as a sort of warning sign, an omen from the universe, and even if that sign was hard to read, my fiancé's lack of care and comfort—not to mention his warning that he'd abandon me—was not.

So now I've managed to stay calm, which has to be a good omen.

Toward the end of the silent retreat, I begin to feel as if I have an altered sense of awareness of everything around me. After I finish reading one novel I don't start any of the five others I've brought, not wanting to take myself out of the experience anymore but instead trying to stay in a state of constant mindfulness that feels a little like being on acid—noticing everything around me with a sense of benevolent amazement, moving amid nature and other people with a quiet ease and grace.

With nothing else to do, I spend a lot of time in the sessions doing the lovingkindness meditation. At first, after giving myself some cursory kindness, I quickly move on to others. But as I have so many long hours to meditate, I might as well pause and give myself a little more time to say May I be safe, May I be happy, May I be healthy, May I live in ease, May I love and be loved. The longer I say these things to myself, the more I feel my heart cracking open. This is such an unusual voice for me. Usually I say You're so stupid, You make foolish mistakes, You can't be trusted, You blew it, You're such a bitch sometimes, You're middle-aged and chubby, even with all that fucking exercise you do, You swear too much, and You're never going to be loved. No wonder I so often feel frantic to escape from myself.

So I sit there offering myself lovingkindness, over and over, luxuriating in it, basking in a sense of well-being. Then when I turn to offer lovingkindness to other people in my life, it's bathed in more golden happy intention. I start with people who are easy, who love me, whom I'm grateful for, people like my parents and sisters, Maya and Cecilia, Sandra, Giovanna, and Kathy; my guy friends; all the people at the writers' collective where I work. I realize, going through my friends with my wishes, how I am grateful to have so many (especially since the meditation session is so long). I offer lovingkindness to people in difficult straits, the sex-trafficked women in Italy, women coffee workers I met in Nicaragua. I work my way to neutral people, like the people on the retreat, and then move on to difficult people. I start with my roommate in the Guatemalan pants, and when I'm feeling compassionate for her, I tackle a few mismatched relationships and bad dates—they probably didn't mean to be so difficult or harsh. Finally I offer it up to my ex-husband and, in the end, to the Samoan surfer, who did, after all, apologize. May he be safe from sharks. Or at least recover from being tossed around and severely bitten.

On the last day we break the silence, and people begin talking to one another about their experience. The guy I developed a silent crush on, fantasizing about his boyfriend potential—an interesting-looking dark-haired man with silver streaks in his hair—turns out not to have a very nice voice or manner, which tells you something about crushes and projection in general and why it's often a good idea not to act right away on your lustful impulses. I leave the chattering group, unable to handle all that human noise or to ask the others their names, where they live, what they do, or how long they've been meditating. I fold my things and leave the retreat center quietly, saying a few words of appreciation to the people I spent the week mopping floors with in the kitchen, people who had done that dirty job efficiently, cheerfully, and well.

Then I get into my car, put the top down, and drive through the redwoods to Point Reyes National Seashore. It is early, so I go on a hike, climbing up Mount Wittenberg to the place where you can look out at the whole peninsula, the westernmost spot in the continental United States, which is edging up the San Andreas Fault at something like six inches per year. This is the spot where I sat several years ago and watched a mountain lion on a hill directly across from me, with a safe valley between us, and knew he was watching me, too. A special spot. Beyond the wildflowers and ferns and rolling stands of pine trees are the long beach, rocky cliffs, and lighthouse in the distance. I feel a contented sense that as much as I love to travel, as much as I am always searching for something somewhere else, there is no place I like being better in the world than in Point Reyes. I feel no urgency to be anywhere else.

On the way out of the park I stop in a small shop in Inverness, to dip back into human company. I look at some pretty things without a desire to buy them and greet the shopkeeper. She asks where I've come from, and I tell her I just spent ten days at Spirit Rock on a silent retreat. "That must be why you have this amazing glow about you," she says. I beam a smile, then go sit in a restaurant garden and thoroughly appreciate a cool pale ale.

Back home in San Francisco, other people notice a change as well. At a party, a man who has known me for twenty years, with whom I've had a tumultuous and long-ago steamy relationship, wants to know what is different about me and tells me I seem "softer." I don't think anyone has ever called me soft before. Kathy, on a hike, is full of sympathetic joy for all the happy revelations I've made. I manage to maintain this peaceful aura for weeks, even on a trip to stressful, fast-paced, career-anxious New York City. There I visit an editor I've known for years, who'd been on staff at a magazine where I once had an altercation with another editor and imprudently used the F-word, a sin for which I was forever banned from those pages, even though I'd been a longtime contributor. "You seem changed," she tells me. "Quieter, calmer, more relaxed. It's nice."

After the meditation retreat, I *am* nice, which ordinarily is not one of the first words even my dearest friends would use to describe me, but I realize that lovely state of sweetness and calm wears off if you don't renew it by meditating some more. Otherwise, you start yelling in traffic again, screaming at some asshole who can't hear you to Learn to Fucking Drive. Meditation, unfortunately, is not like a vaccine against impulsiveness, it's more like exercise, which you have to do at least a few times a week in order not to slip back into your old irritable, impatient self. That's why they call it practice.

I probably can't get that lovely beatific glow back, where children, rattlesnakes, and strangers are drawn to my preternatural goodness and calmed by my presence, not without another ten-day silent retreat. But I can sit a few minutes a few days a week to make sure my pause button still works.

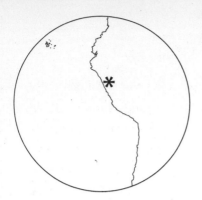

I n the midst of all that meditating, I nearly forget I am on a campaign to find a boyfriend by forty-five, when I will be officially middle-aged. It seems to have lost its urgency. Meditation does seem to help me deal with men; all my encounters seem less dramatic and personally corrosive.

When I start dating Evan, it is easier to let go of my usual anxieties about whether he likes me enough, has all the necessary characteristics I need in a partner, and whether we are going to end up happily ever after. I can appreciate who he is, full of sunny energy, enjoy taking a hike with him and his dog, and make dinner later on, not worrying so much about how or if things will develop. I have a little space to check in with myself for a change—what's up with this guy, how does he make me feel?—not just react to how I think he is thinking about me. I am less judgmental about him and simply notice him, whether I really want him to be my boyfriend or whether I'll have to continue my campaign.

After we've been dating a couple of months, I land an assignment to go to Peru to write about its new, hot cuisine with my friend Guillermo. Evan isn't exactly jealous that I'm going with Guillermo—I tell him the truth, which is that we're strictly friends—but he isn't thrilled either. I remind Evan that he said he wanted to travel with me and invite him to meet up with me in Peru after Guillermo leaves. To my surprise, since he has traveled very little outside the United States, he immediately agrees.

Guillermo, who is Peruvian, cooked up an idea with me to eat our way around Lima's best restaurants and have a magazine foot the bill. Since he left the country, during the era of the Shining Path terrorism, Peru's varied cuisines have become more sophisticated, mostly as a result of some young chefs who departed around that same time and returned with new, European-inspired techniques and an urge to rediscover traditional dishes and ingredients that ranged from the Andes to the Amazon.

Guillermo is excited to return to Peru after many years and writes to all his friends for suggestions about great restaurants. Meanwhile, Evan and I research an adventure company to take us on the Inca Trail and figure out where to go in the Amazon. I try to pack clothes for fine dining, high-altitude trekking, and the steamy jungle in one bag.

Finally, the day arrives when I meet Guillermo at the airport and we fly to Lima. We rent a little Jeep and drive to his mother's house, a formal, immaculate haven in chaotic Lima. I'm glad to be with Guillermo, who knows the city and is so aware of its dangers that he won't let me get out of the car until he opens the door for me, so he can be by my side.

We begin our mission to eat at restaurants that tell the story of Peru's history in their dishes, starting with a visit to the restaurant owned by one of Guillermo's childhood friends who is now Peru's most famous chef. We try ceviche of wild sea bass with lime and red onions, which tells the tale of people who have long caught fish in the morning and had a taboo against eating it later than lunch. We taste a tiradito, sliced raw bonito, an interpretation of Peru's nikkei, or second-generation Japanese, cuisine, along with sea urchins on tender ribbons of raw calamari. We have spicy chifa food in a downtown Chinese restaurant. We snack on anticuchos—beef-heart kebabs—from streetside carts. We stuff ourselves with stuffed peppers from Arequipa's *picantería* cuisine and with risotto with black scallops that speak of the African-inflected *criollo* food still served in most homes. We eat roasted guinea pig, albeit an organic one, nestled in a bed of oca ravioli in a pisco pecan sauce. We even try a tough piece of alpaca.

By the time we leave Lima, heading south for Arequipa, we are ill, unable to stomach the thought of food. We can only barely appreciate Arequipa's gorgeous city-within-a-city, the Convent of Santa Catalina, where wealthy nuns lived lavishly, painting their walls in exquisite colors, decorating with simple but impeccable taste, surrounding themselves with colonial masterpieces. We are only slightly recovered when we drive over high-altitude dirt roads to the Colca Canyon to chase after condors and sit in hot springs. Guillermo, being a Peruvian, with an endless thirst for information about history, geography, and ethnography, is a wonderful companion and guide. One of the good things about not being married is that you can be friends with men whom for whatever reason you aren't lovers with—in Guillermo's case, maybe the fact that we have the same birthday makes us astrological siblings, too much alike, but we both agree we are best off being friends, so there has never been any tension. For whatever bad luck I've had with men in the romance realm, I can't overlook, and probably wouldn't trade, my great fortune in having lasting friendships with wonderful men.

After Guillermo goes home, Evan meets me in Lima with a burst of excited energy. We've been planning our Peru adventure almost since the time we started dating a few months before. Evan, an engineer, prepared for our trip meticulously, with geological and topographical maps, a GPS gadget, several guidebooks, and two duffel bags filled with wicking, water-repellant, bug-off layers of clothing for every climate emergency (we're going from the Amazon to the Andes). He is taking care of all the details, and everything is under control. He printed a spreadsheet listing reservation numbers, transportation times, and contacts, as well as things we should remember to have available in our day packs each day. This is a marked contrast to the way I usually travel or with Guillermo, since we'd prepared only by soliciting restaurant recommendations, casually changing modes from lunch with a count in the oldest home in the Americas (Guillermo is a fortuneless Peruvian aristocrat) to walking around fields, talking to Indians about their crops.

Once organized, Evan is game and easygoing. We fly to a town in the Amazon and take a boat up a steamy river to a jungle exploration center, where we stay in a hut and traipse around the lush and overwhelming jungle, feeling Lilliputian, listening for monkeys, and watching out for snakes. While we're there I think about the story Guillermo told me about his father, whose helicopter crashed in the jungle when he was three; when they found his body, they estimated he'd managed to stay alive a month before the insects and jungle diseases overcame him, which is one reason Guillermo has a mania for survival skills. The jungle is inhospitable in the extreme.

Evan, too, is a capable companion, and I feel safe traveling with him. We take a boat trip farther up the river, camp out, and wake at dawn to cross the river with a machete-wielding guide, then wait for a skittish gathering of birds at a clay wall, finally peering out from behind a blind at the brilliant sight of thousands of bright green and red macaws. It is the best adventure you could wish to have with any partner.

That night, on our return, the people who run the jungle center offer us another journey, with a local shaman, taking ayahuasca, a sacred plant that induces visions, used in local healing ceremonies. I have an anthropologist friend who has done quite a bit of research on the hallucinogenic vine, bringing scientists down to see how the ancient drug reveals the very structure of DNA in visions, so naturally I am curious. Since one isn't often in the Amazon jungle with the opportunity to join an ayahuasca ceremony with a shaman, I decide to participate. Evan isn't interested; he tried a few psychedelics when he was younger and says he knows all he wants to know about that particular path to those territories of his brain. He goes off to have a few reliable beers with an Englishman who is likewise staying at our camp.

Undeterred, I sign up for the ceremony alone. The shaman,

an elderly Indian man in sharply creased jeans, arrives on a little boat around sunset. We gather in one of the huts—a few of the employees, a couple other guests, and the shaman—and scatter ourselves on mattresses on the floor. I dimly realize that I haven't followed the first rule of taking psychedelics, which is set and setting, meaning a positive frame of mind, a comfortable place, people you trust. I don't know these people, much less anything about the shaman or his ayahuasca, and though my mind is calm and untroubled, my body is still recovering from one of the low-grade bugs that gnaw on your GI tract for much of the time you spend in Peru, no matter what you do. Still, when the shaman offers me a cup of vile brown liquid, I down it, fast.

I know that ayahuasca, like peyote or mescaline, acts as an emetic, but I figure it will just make me burp, tidily empty the contents of my tummy, and then I'll be ready for the visions the shaman is conducting, open to whatever revelations about self, nature, the universe, and the oneness of them all that the vine is willing to offer. What I don't expect is four hours of psychedelic barfing. My skin becomes clammy, I have a tweaky sensation around my jaw, someone hands me a bag, and I begin my first round. It isn't disgusting, exactly, but curious; I intently notice everything, as if vomiting in slow motion, the sound of the crinkling bag heightened, the expulsions colorful, my physical sensations coming from afar. The shaman, who is whistling, makes soothing sounds every time I retch. At some point, when I can close my eyes long enough not to have to aim into the bag again, I have visions, like a rolling, writhing picture of the jungle, which I could have seen had I just stepped outside the door and twirled

around until I was dizzy. Given my recent gastrointestinal dis-
tress, I am distracted from these transcendent visions by an im-
manent need to use the bathroom, which, though only a few steps
away, might as well be across the piranha-infested river for all I
am able to move.

Finally, when I cough up the last bilious drops from my stomach, dry heaving for good measure, the visions stop, my intestines
settle down, and I take a nap on the mattress. I am chilly, and all I
can think about is how I want someone next to me, someone who
will hold me close and take care of me. It is a desire that is much
bigger than the moment and, in my state, seems profound. When I
wake, I make it back to our hut, finally use the bathroom, shower,
and toothbrush, and crawl under the mosquito netting with Evan.
I cuddle up to him. "I like you this way," he says. "You should
take that vine stuff more often." He is drunk and chatty about his
evening with the English guy, and somehow I don't feel the deep
closeness I need—the one strong message the ayahuasca managed
to deliver—but I'm glad to have him spoon me to sleep.

In the morning I am renewed; I have a ferocious appetite
for breakfast, and whatever bug has been dogging me since Arequipa has been decidedly driven away. The shaman tells me that
though I shouldn't have taken the ayahuasca when I was still ill,
now surely the bug is cleaned out—the healers use it in small
doses to rid people of amoebas and parasites. We leave that lush
and mysterious world on the same boat to town and then take
a bus to the airport, where Evan and I depart for Cuzco, flying
over a dozen microclimates in a short hour, from deepest jungle
to high arid desert.

Cuzco is a spectacular city, red rooftops surrounded by high, rugged mountains. Its colonial houses remind me of what I remember of San Miguel de Allende in the high desert of Mexico, though the buildings are older and more imposing for their enormous hand-hewn stones. We explore the town and nearby ruins, eating in colonial haciendas, ex-monasteries, and modern art museums. After spending time with Guillermo, who travels light and is as fast to get up and go as I am, it is difficult to adjust to Evan's pace: when I'm ready to head out the door, he has another forty-five minutes left of organizing his gear. You always have to compromise when you travel with someone, so I write postcards or explore the gift shop, but when he is willing to skip the Sacred Valley and Ollantaytombo, perhaps Peru's second greatest ruins, to save taxi fare and be sure we are back in time to pick up our laundry, I say I'd like to go and he can join me if he likes, which he does.

THE NEXT MORNING we take the train to hike the Inca Trail, with our guide, Narciso, an easygoing and dry-humored Inca descendent who is an amateur anthropologist. From the first day on that ancient trail, passing ruins and villages, ascending into the high Andes, we are awed by the experience. Along with nuggets of history and mythology, Narciso passes out coca leaves to villagers we see along the trail and to our group, to help us with altitude sickness and to give us energy (I am not interested in trying any more local drugs). Evan and I snuggle in our tent during the cold nights and encourage each other up the difficult trail.

We climb up the highest point, Abra de Huarmihuanusca, Dead Woman's Pass, more than 13,000 feet high, and marvel at the view. On the last morning, we wake at sunrise to watch the dawn hit the Cordillera Blanca, the white-topped mountains, including the 20,500-foot Nevado Salkantay. Evan is elated at the morning and greets it bare-chested, arms raised in an animal howl of appreciation. At that moment, I am crazy about him. That last day, when we finally climb the ancient, tidy stones to the Inti Punku, the Gateway to the Sun, we are both wonderstruck by the sight of Machu Picchu—that something so grand could exist in such an astonishing setting, that human beings could create and inhabit such a magical space—me with tears rolling down my cheeks, him giving me a big bear hug.

"You're wonderful to travel with," I tell him.

"This is easy," he says. "It's being together at home that's difficult."

ONCE BACK IN the Bay Area, photos developed and organized with scanned topographical maps, then put away, I realize he is right. Evan has a fun streak on vacation and on the weekends—when, superenergetic, he's happy to dance, take bike rides, make love, and head out skiing—but his week is all routine. He microwaves his Lean Pocket at a precise time each morning, watches sports highlights for a few minutes, catches the bus to work, comes home, gets stoned, walks his dog, and crashes. Anything that breaks his regimen—going out to dinner, staying at my house—is a hassle. Still, as much as I like every day to be

its own little unpredictable journey, I also appreciate the stability
and regularity of someone to sleep with, to help me put up shelves
in my office. At a certain point we talk about moving in together,
and he cheerfully appoints me Director of Aesthetics, saying I can
toss whatever of his postcollege furniture I like as long as he has
a corner of his own to work in. We'll live in my flat, he says, until
we can buy a place we can afford, probably outside the city, where
we'll have a dog, maybe adopt a kid, and he'll take a longer bus
ride into the city every day. Since that seems like a distant day to
me (and I am very fond of the city), I am willing, in the meantime,
to empty a sock drawer for him and talk about getting cable.

So I have managed what I said I wanted before I hit forty-
five: a man who is interested in building a life with me, with all
the trimmings of successful middle age—child, dog, and house in
the suburbs. But the nine months of our relationship are starting
to feel like nine years. We are no longer making love so avidly,
with the red tango shoes on, but complain of being tired before
we roll over, facing different directions. Though I thought our
trip to Peru was the first of many adventures to come, I now realize it was the first and last foreign trip he'd take in many years.
Instead, he is committed to seeing his parents in Florida for most
of his annual two weeks' vacation time, and though he insists that
I join him, he makes it clear that it will be no fun.

"My mother is going to hate you," Evan says over dinner one
evening when we are discussing the trip.

"Great," I say. "Why?" Normally, I'm good with parents—
polite and interested in them, and I write charming thank-you
notes on cream-colored stationery.

"You're not Jewish, you're not a lawyer, and you're probably too old to have children," Evan says.

"Well," I say. If I had known those were the qualifications for the job, I would not have applied. I will leave it to him to figure out with a shrink why he is dating a woman with precisely all the attributes his mother would hate. "There's not much I can do about any of that."

It is far too late to start trying to be someone else for the sake of a man. This isn't the first time I've been called a shiksa, and it annoys me: if a Jewish guy is interested in me, as happens rather more often than demographics would suggest is proportionate, for whatever reason, that's his issue to debate with himself and not my fault for luring him away. I'm too old to apologize for being who I am, a zaftig shiksa with a fair dose of chutzpah. Anyway, we WASPs don't believe in guilt.

"If we got married, my mother wouldn't come to the wedding," says Evan.

This is the first time the phrase "if we got married" has popped out of his mouth, and I decide to ignore it for the time being. My first marriage demystified the glories of connubial bliss, and though I am eager for companionship, I am in no hurry to repeat any major mistakes. Plus it doesn't seem like a good sign that the first time he's bringing it up it's negative, a problem already.

"So your mother will hate me but you want me to come to Florida to visit her anyway?"

"She's my mom. It's important to me."

"Right." I'm not sure what's going to happen between us, but I know I'm not going to visit sunny Florida anytime soon. There are compromises that you make for your man, and then there is masochism.

FOR OUR BIRTHDAYS, his forty-second and my forty-fifth, Guillermo and I throw a Peruvian fiesta, celebrating our recent trip. We—mostly he—make aji de gallina, a peppery chicken stew, Peruvian tamales, and a trio of causas, piles of cold mashed potatoes topped with olives, fish, and sauces; his sister whips up a soufflé of lucuma, a Peruvian fruit that tastes like sweet Thai iced tea and is reason enough to visit that country. We pour pisco sours and celebrate our friendships; I clink glasses too with Evan, who, a couple of days before my actual birthday, I can say is my boyfriend, even though the thought lurks that you have to be careful what you campaign for.

The Peruvian birthday party is a big success, everyone complimenting the food and the photos of the trip. Guillermo has made perfect pisco sours with a little egg foam on top. Evan is his usual gregarious self, all my friends tell me how it seems as though they've known him for years, we have a rousing romp at the end of the evening, and I go to bed happy to be forty-five, or at least satisfied that I've arrived at middle age in good spirits.

My actual birthday is two days later, and I have plans to meet Evan at my favorite kind of place, a southern Italian–style trattoria with locally grown food and an honest wine list. I go to a yoga class and am feeling balanced and flexible. When Evan shows up at the restaurant, late, he is carrying a Hallmark bag covered in pink roses.

I open my present. Inside is a bar of chocolate. A large bar, to be fair. It is not, though, Turkish gold earrings, tickets to an Elvis Costello concert, the new Murakami novel, or a CD of love songs he compiled just for me. It is not even artisanal French chocolate or Fair Trade single-estate 72% cacao. It is not any of the words that go perfectly well with "forty-fifth birthday," "girlfriend," and "present." But it is dark chocolate, which is my favorite. I thank him, lift my glass, and focus on the tiny prosecco bubbles.

I'm not quite sure what turn the conversation takes between the appetizers and the main dish. I know I get pensive around birthdays, trying to sort out the big picture—what do I want in life, who are we together, have we examined all the red flags, why don't you like broccoli rabe with anchovies—but somewhere two-thirds of the way into the Barbera, I hear Evan say, "Maybe we should just break up." He isn't asking for my opinion.

That definitely isn't the way I imagined things: breaking up on a birthday—a multiple-of-five birthday, no less—over dinner, in public. I can't believe it's happening. But there he is, moving his mouth, apologizing, saying he is just a guy, I'll find a better one, none of his relationships lasts long, it isn't the end of the world, it just didn't work out, we aren't in love. All of this is undeniably true, no matter how I might have tried to see it otherwise, but it is my birthday, my forty-fifth f—ing birthday, the finish line in my campaign to better myself—and I don't like having those particular facts pointed out right now.

When the server approaches the table, I am embarrassed that tears are rolling down my cheeks, pooling into my new coral satin bra—which, now, no one will admire (and which cost the equivalent of forty big bars of chocolate).

"I'm sorry," I tell the waitress in Italian, which Evan does not speak. She gives me a kind smile and a shrug. *"Non fa niente,"* she says. It's nothing.

"Can you believe," I go on, trying to explain why I have completely lost it over the excellent milk-fed pork, "that this stronzo is breaking up with me? On my forty-fifth birthday?"

"Him?" she replies, pushing back her black curls. Without skipping a beat: "I thought he was gay."

I retreat to the restroom to wash my face, and when I return, she's put a piece of serious dark chocolate cake on the table, with a candle. This is one of those occasions when you can rely on both Italians and really good dark bitter chocolate—not a big bar of grocery store chocolate—to comfort and cheer you. "He's not worth it, *cara,*" she says. "You'll find someone better."

Evan reaches his fork over for a bite of the cake, but I intercept, push it away, cut him a sliver, and place it on his plate. There will be no more sharing from the same dish. There will be no more living with jock talk in the morning and no more moving to the suburbs. I realize I am going to miss his dog. I tell Evan we could be friends, which I know probably won't turn out to be true, and blow out the candle.

But what can I wish for? I'm forty-five. Game over, time's up. My boyfriend—my last hope for some conventional semblance of adult life—has just broken up with me. I don't know if I'll ever have another relationship—or sex, for that matter—again.

But what did Sandra say on my last birthday? Nothing expires until you do. I may not have succeeded in my campaign to find a husband and cozy stability, but I have succeeded in realizing that at least this version of that goal isn't really what I wanted.

The year and the campaign have hardly been a total waste. If I learned anything from tango, it's to be alert and receptive and not jump to any conclusions. And if I've understood anything from meditating, it's that all we have is the present and all we can do is appreciate the moment, not live with an eye to the future, full of attachment and desire, or regret about the past.

So I make some wishes to be safe, to be happy, to be healthy, to love and be loved. Then I take a few moments to offer those wishes to many people I'm grateful for in my life. Even Evan.

And then I take a big bite of rich, warm, intense, slightly bitter chocolate cake.

I CHECK MY e-mail before going to bed. "Candle," is the subject line, an e-mail from France, from the Professor, wishing that la bella vita continues this year, sending me "kisses and so and so." And *that* is a sweet birthday present.

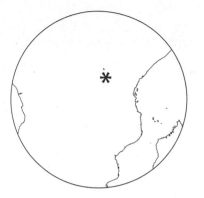

Despite my efforts to be cheerful, or at least full of Buddhist equanimity, things are a bit bleak after I break up with Evan. I can't help feeling blue about the unfortunate timing, as if the universe were pointing out that he was my last-ditch hope for a partner and family, comfort and stability, before my youth expired. It makes sense that we split up, but it doesn't make sense that I am single, with zero prospects. Even though I feel a distinct sense of relief after he's gone, it still bothers me that I didn't manage to be patient and receptive enough to attract a man who would travel the world with me, holding my hand and watching out for pickpockets. Each time I break up with someone, I have to admit that he wasn't right for me, but the disappointment is that once again he was the wrong guy. And even though men seem to arrive in my life like trains pulling into a station with no schedule, unpredictably, yet eventually, when I'm standing there alone on the tracks with the last one disappearing out of sight, I never believe I'll see another.

The Monday after that miserable forty-fifth-birthday breakup

I go to my office, a writers' collective that I share with a group of freelance writers and filmmakers. I hole up in a black mood, not interested in seeing my colleagues, even though they are invariably full of lively lunch conversation about writing and politics and can be counted on to compliment my haircut or shoes. In the middle of the afternoon the doorbell rings, and I drag myself to answer it.

It is Gustavo. I haven't seen or heard from him since the last time I left his bed. I am shocked; he is the last person I want to see in my present state. He wasn't expecting to see me, either, since he is there to meet a filmmaker. I look like hell, my heart is sore from my recent breakup, and I've just gotten an extremely short haircut as a sort of Fuck Men reaction to events. It isn't what I need, to run into this beefy, dark-haired Brazilian with his sly smile, reminding me that things never work out and that I will probably never have sex that good again in my life, if I ever manage to have sex again at all.

Gustavo hugs me and politely asks how I am doing. "I just turned forty-five and broke up with my boyfriend," I blurt, giving him too much information, especially since he might not otherwise have guessed precisely how much older than he I am. I try to recover with a lame laugh. "Good thing it's a new week." I hold it together and we chat briefly; he's just been in Brazil to see his girlfriend, the dark-haired beauty whose photo I conveniently ignored when I spent the night at his apartment, and they are finally moving in together. I am glad at least that all that talent isn't going to waste.

"Are you going to be all right?" he asks, his eyes briefly searching mine.

"Sure," I say, looking away. "Take it easy."

I really am not all right. My European, *joie de vivre* attitude about food and wine is turning into overeating and drinking to bloated grogginess every evening. I stop meditating, as if willing myself down a black hole. I am listless, writing whatever any magazine editor calls up and suggests I write—about an interior designer in San Diego who makes creative use of ottomans, the five best budget hotels in San Francisco, the Queen of Organic Greens— and have zero ideas of my own. The bottom comes when I agree to do a slick women's magazine story on "stumbling blocks to women's friendships," thinking it is a personal essay I can whip out quickly, but instead the editor wants me to interview random but demographically balanced and zip code–diverse women about their myriad issues with female friends. I just can't make myself do another of those interviews with friends of friends about a vague topic, I can't write another article that starts with a breezy dramatic anecdote, goes on to a nut graf defining a faux trend, then speeds through three more gripping personal stories, each illustrating a different aspect of the supposed trend, finally having a Malibu PhD who recently wrote a peppy self-help book on the subject weigh in with friendly solutions and bullet points so we can all stop thinking about it and go back to shopping already.

I am simply unable, psychologically incapacitated, paralyzed. I have not been so depressed since my husband left me or George W. Bush stole the White House from Al Gore, I'm not sure which.

One afternoon I have coffee in the Mission neighborhood with my friend Trish, whom I met a couple of years ago while doing a story in Nicaragua, where she organizes Fair Trade coffee cooperatives. It was inspiring, to see what a huge difference a puny increase in coffee prices could make to people living in huts without shoes, how it could build health care centers and schools; it was also fun to dance salsa and soak in hot springs in view of a volcano. All that seems very far away now. Trish is still traveling to coffee countries but is now packing up her entire life and moving to the East Coast to be with an international development expert she happened to meet and fall in love with. It won't slow her down: she will travel out of Dulles instead of SFO, meeting in exotic locales with her fiancé, who also travels frequently, and I'm glad she seems happy, having sorted things out after forty, able to retain her independence and love of travel and still have a committed relationship with someone.

Over steaming lattes, I confess how depressed I am, how I have no prospects in romance or work, no energy to come up with ideas or do much of anything except stay home at night and devour DVDs, as if consuming culture were the same as creating it.

Trish suggests I should go to Rwanda if I am so depressed. At first I think that is a surprisingly scolding, unfunny remark: if you want to make yourself feel better about having a midlife crisis, go take a look at the aftermath of genocide, that'll put things into perspective. It is true, of course, that in the big scheme of things I have absolutely nothing to complain about and everything to be grateful for, but nevertheless it seems extreme, and maybe self-righteous, to bring up Rwanda in the context of our conversation.

But Trish is serious. She is leading a trip to Rwanda for coffee importers and tells me that if I pay my own way, I can come along. Surely, she says, you can find some sort of a story to write from Rwanda.

That gives me reason to wake up the next morning, rouses my inner Brenda Starr, and less than a month later, I find myself arriving at the airport in Kigali, Rwanda.

IN THE INTERVENING weeks I have read everything I could find about Rwanda and the 1994 genocide there, but nothing has prepared me for being in that tragic and beautiful country and encountering its people and ghosts. I have never been to Africa before and only stopped off en route to spend a few days in the still-colonial tourist enclaves of Nairobi and at a posh game resort to do a travel article to help pay my way (astonished, as everyone is, that the elephants, zebras, water buffalo, and lion cubs roam around just as they do on the National Geographic Channel). So arriving in Rwanda, the most densely populated country on the continent and one of the poorest, is a shock. I expected the shacks and barefoot children—I've seen poverty like that in Latin America—but I am surprised to see so many lush hills and to meet brightly dressed people whose ready smiles gave little hint of their history.

I meet up with Trish and the rest of her group, including a sociology professor, his students, and a couple of coffee importers. We spend our first days in and around Kigali, touring the sites of the genocide—at a million deaths in a hundred days, one of the most brutal episodes in human history. I have been to Yad Vashem in Jerusalem, and Rwanda's memorial sites are as

chilling and horrifying, perhaps for being more recent, the genocide having taken place only a dozen years before, during my
adult lifetime and the Clinton administration, to its everlasting
shame. We visit one brick church where thousands of Tutsis
sought shelter from the rampaging Hutus and nearly all were
massacred. There are bullet holes in the altar and enormous crypts
in the back filled with boxes of bones and row upon row of skulls,
lined up like books in an enormous library. At another church,
women's pocketbooks are still left behind in the pews, scattered
among teenage T-shirts and baby shoes, those small daily objects
more heartbreaking, somehow, than all the skulls.

I am astonished by our upbeat translator, Alice, who is in her
early twenties, whose entire family was killed while she was away
at day school and whose uncle was massacred while she watched
from where she was hiding. She is able to relate the history of the
genocide calmly, as if it didn't happen before her eyes. The only
time she becomes emotional is when she tells the story of a boy
who grew up with her in an orphanage. While standing in front
of the church where these events happened, she describes how the
boy's Tutsi mother threw her baby out of the church to a Hutu
woman when the Hutu militia started shelling the building. The
woman held on to the baby, but the Hutu soldiers recognized that
it wasn't hers and threw it back into the burning church. The
woman dashed into the church, rescued the baby, and ran back
out to safety, initially taking the boy to the orphanage where
Alice grew up, afraid of reprisal if she kept it herself. Eventually
she adopted him and raised him, with mixed ethnicities, as his
mother. Alice wipes tears from her eyes—the only time I see her
cry—from her happy-ending story.

The next day Alice takes me to visit the Rwanda Widows' Association to interview the director, a genocide widow herself. This group, in its plain and tidy offices, has an insurmountable task—trying to give psychological, economic, medical, and social support to the widows left from the genocide, more than two-thirds of whom were raped and half of those left HIV-positive by their attackers. The stigma surrounding rape left the women unable to testify in the local *gacaca* courts, which attempted a sort of village-level justice for the genocide, so the association offers surrogates. Many of the survivors gave birth to babies fathered by their rapists and either gave them away or had to cope with their older children taunting the younger ones, "Your father killed my father." Others have no other children left. Some of the women live in dire poverty, in a situation where, with their husbands dead, they can't own land. "We live like ghosts," the director tells me. "Our lives are over, and we only keep going for our children."

The woman, so full of dignity, almost begs me to publicize the plight of the Rwandan widows. "The world has stopped giving economic aid to these women because they say that the emergency is over," she tells me. Journalist or not, I empty my pockets on the way out and promise her I'll do my best. (When at home I pitch the story to several magazines, I get the same response from all of them: the emergency is over, the genocide is old news.)

From Kigali, our group drives through rolling green hills, densely populated with villages, to a resort that serves as a staging area for treks to see the silverback gorillas of Dian Fossey fame. We encounter these massive and playful creatures face-to-face the next day, and they are an impressive, once-in-a-lifetime sight but an odd juxtaposition to the genocide tour (so much public out-pouring of concern for those endangered gorillas, so little for the widows). I share a room with Alice, who wakes up screaming in the middle of the night, and it overwhelms me to realize that she always wakes up screaming in the night and that there is no pos-sible way to comfort her, only to leave the lights on, hug her, and say that we are safe, there is no reason to be afraid. The worst has already happened to her.

We go on to Butare, where we meet people who work in a coffee project that is markedly improving the circumstances of the local growers. A charismatic and visionary American agri-culture professor set up a program to help the Rwandans process their high-quality coffee beans to sell to the gourmet market, at many times the price of what they'd been selling in bulk to the big-can companies. Rwandans have a long history of being forced to grow coffee, mostly by colonial Belgians who beat them if they refused to comply, so it was a complicated task to get Rwandans to care about growing coffee (because of their brutal past, most Rwandans prefer to drink tea). But by building clean, landscaped washing and sorting stations for the coffee, which serve as a kind of community center for the villagers, the program created an atmosphere where women whose husbands were killed in the genocide can work side by side with women whose husbands are in prison for the crimes. "Reconciliation" is the word repeatedly used by the nongovernmental organization workers and politi-cians we met to talk about progress in Rwanda, but this is a real example, former enemies working together for a common eco-nomic good. I'm astonished at the resiliency of these women, who can cooperate under the most humanly unlikely circumstances and create new stability for themselves together.

The village is prospering; a new hair salon and restaurant have popped up, along with an Internet café sponsored by the coffee program. Some people have wooden bikes to haul their coffee the long distances to the washing stations, instead of carrying large baskets on their heads. It is, amazingly, a genuine good-news story from Rwanda.

I send a postcard to Maya in Nevada, who will be so eager to hear about these optimistic, grassroots projects with women in Africa, and I can't wait to tell her about them the next time I see her.

The optimistic feeling of the project dims later in the day, when we arrive at the hotel where we are staying in Butare, which has an intensely creepy vibe. I go with Helen, the owner of a coffee company, to check out which rooms we want to stay in, but each one scares us. Without speaking, we agree that we are going to share a room, to stay together. The rooms are simple and tidy, with an innocuous bed, table, and chair, but something about each makes us too uncomfortable to stay. We finally settle on one, and, though there are two beds, we decide to sleep together, to feel safe.

"My one time in bed with a lesbian, and nothing happens," I joke with Helen, trying to lighten the mood.

(I later read that there was a reason the hotel rooms felt so creepy. Butare had initially been a relative haven during the genocide, because the prefect was Tutsi and it had the largest Tutsi population in the country; but the government sent in militia groups from Kigali to begin the massacre, starting with the eighty-year-old widow of the former Tutsi ruler, moving on to professors and students at the university, then to the hospital, and working systematically through the neighborhoods, convincing the locals to kill or be killed. The headquarters of the engineers of what became one of the worst massacres of the genocide was the hotel where we stayed. The arboretum where we'd taken an afternoon walk had been one of the biggest killing grounds.)

The atmosphere in Butare is so grim that Helen and I both want to leave as fast as possible; I take a bus back to Kigali for a flight the next day, and she is sorry to see me go without her. By then I have my story, including interviews Alice helped me get with some genocide survivors who are growing coffee and a long list of other sources. I tell the group over our last dinner together that it seems like it could be a good business story, maybe for the *New York Times*—an example of economic growth and reconciliation in a poverty-stricken, landlocked African country, still simmering with ethnic tensions but moving forward nonetheless—and though the women in the group make encouraging noises, the sociology professor gives me a skeptical look. I am a women's magazine writer who wrote a memoir about sex and food in Italy, for God's sake. Lightweight.

At home I procrastinate for a while and think about sending the article to the local paper. I hate the thought of proposing the story to the *Times* and having it ignore my e-mail, which is probably what will happen. I'd feel like a total loser. But I am hardly the point: the story deserves a wider audience, and it isn't as if an omniscient editor at the *Times* knows I've been to Rwanda and have a good piece and is going to call me up and *ask* me to send it in. I have to risk feeling like an idiot, the person the sociology professor mocked, and so, what the hell—I'm a grown-up, I'm forty-five—I pitch the story to the business editor of the Sunday *Times*. He e-mails back one line: "How fast can I say yes?"

I spend three more weeks reporting on the Rwandan coffee industry, get a quote from everyone including President Paul Kagame, and the piece sails through the *Times* editing process, handled by some of the most cordial professionals I've ever worked with. It ends up on the front page of the Sunday business section, with a beautiful photo of Rwandan women sorting coffee cherries, and shortly thereafter, the coffee group, whose funding had been endangered, receives a new grant, thanks in part, the director tells me, to the reporting. The check from the *Times* just covers my expenses for the trip; I use it to send Alice winter clothes and a computer for graduate school in Canada, to which she received a scholarship. (Helen and her partner, who are childless, have since supported Alice like parents, and I've done my best to be a big sister.)

The story lifts me out of my funk, wakes me up, and, just as my friend Trish guessed that day over coffee, gives me a wider perspective on the world and the work I could be doing. It's not the kind of experience that's easy to duplicate, but it raises the bar, expands the possibilities.

When I get home, I get the news that Maya has passed away. That seems impossible to me, because she was just here, maybe ninety but with such a strong spirit. I go to the ranch and can hardly stand to be there without her; I keep expecting to come upon her soaking in the hot tub or reading a book in her big kitchen. At her memorial, hundreds of people arrive, telling tearful tales about her impact on their lives, through politics or friendship or as a grandmother. She lived a full life, and at the end, along with her family, had a huge circle of friends for companionship. I stay on a few days at the ranch, in her quiet house, but I miss her offering me a glass of wine and asking if I've written my thousand words yet today. The day I leave, I pick up the mail from down the dirt road, walk back to the house, and find my postcard from Rwanda.

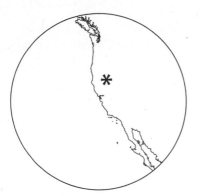

Midway through my forty-sixth year, with no more campaign to try to fix my life by a deadline, I feel less urgency to try to settle down with someone. It's not that I want companionship and stability any less, but I have more of a sense of calm, like you have when you've run a race, lost, are exhausted, and know you've tried your best. The stakes change. There's no rush to find a man in time to have children. That race is over.

There is a certain grief that comes with that realization, but also some relief. Perhaps if the right man came along I might still adopt, but I'm finished with the frantic search for the father of my children. I don't regret not having kids, usually, because I never would have had other experiences that have made my life so richly textured. I also have nephews and a niece I adore and enjoy swooping in as the crazy aunt who has traveled the world, giving them a glimpse of a different kind of life. In any case, it's the way things turned out.

È così, as they say in Italian.

But other issues up in the air still make me uneasy, such as the fact that I'm still living in the Hippie Apartment in the Haight and my retirement plan comes down to marrying a wealthy man or writing a bestseller (I've done both before, to little avail). For all my independence, I have never felt I had the wherewithal to try to buy a house of my own; financially and otherwise, it's always seemed like a two-person proposition. There's nothing wrong with renting—people in New York and Paris do it all their lives—but at my age there is a nagging sense that you ought to have a place on planet Earth to call your own. I have been in a holding pattern, waiting for a man to come along before I make a move to buy a house or change what, twenty-five years later, is essentially a postcollege lifestyle.

I'm also a little tired of San Francisco, which seems crazy, because on a sunny day—houses dressed up like Victorian ladies out for a stroll, Golden Gate Park blooming, the view from the top of Twin Peaks sweeping a circle around an urban paradise and out to sea, restaurants serving up the freshest, tastiest meals on the continent—there is no place better to be. But on one of the innumerable foggy, heavy-lidded summer days, I am itchy to move my life in a different direction, and it's nothing that going to another country for a week is going to cure.

When one of my friends in the writers' collective suggests we hire a personal coach for a couple of days, I agree to participate, just to get unstuck. The coach will work with us on organizing our time and deadlines and setting goals, which is a challenge for us freelance creative types, insecure procrastinators all.

Martha, the coach, shows up at the office, an imposing redhead in her sixties, full of energy and clear intention despite what would, for most people, be a devastating disability: her hands and limbs are gnarled with rheumatoid arthritis. Clearly none of us is going to get away with easy excuses about our limitations. Naturally we have to go around and talk about what we want from the experience. I'm calmer about that process these days, partly because I actually do want some help getting unstuck but also because these are friends I've worked with, in some cases for ten years, and so it's not as if I'll be revealing how neurotic I am. They already know.

Martha starts by talking about the importance of setting goals and keeping commitments in our lives, to ourselves and to others. She asks us to write down our lifelong purpose and see whether what we're doing day to day, and year to year, helps fulfill that purpose. It sounds self-aggrandizing to talk about purpose, and many in the group have never thought in those terms. I'm one of those lucky people, though, who was never tormented about which direction to go in in life. I knew what I wanted to be when I grew up back when I was in third grade and just set about doing it; it wasn't a choice to become a writer but a necessity.

Purpose is a bit deeper than vocation, though. I've been too embarrassed, since my college application essay, to say out loud that I always hoped to use writing to raise consciousness, as a medium for social change; it sounds very seventies. Still, an astrologer recently took a look at my chart and articulated a similar purpose for me: I was handed gifts of language and communication, she said, and with them a responsibility to use them to benefit others, to bring darkness to light, to illuminate circumstances that otherwise might be left hidden, unnoticed, and unexplained.

(Whether or not I believe in the art, astrologers are frighteningly accurate when they read my chart; the last one took one look and whistled, "Wow, you have trouble staying in relationships, don't you?") Taking inventory, I accomplish my purpose occasionally, recently by writing about women in Naples, Nicaragua, and Rwanda and sometimes by describing the challenges of my personal life to benefit others working their way through similar circumstances—there's no way I'd reveal myself otherwise; I'm too shy. But that purpose gets muddled with my personal issues and campaigns and often detoured when I need to take on work I don't care about to pay my rent.

Purpose is important to keep in mind, especially at midlife, when it's so easy to get mired in routine, when checking e-mail, day to day, seems to take precedence over the big projects and the big picture. My mother was struggling to find purpose when she was in her forties, breaking beyond the social expectation to raise children and moving toward making a broader social contribution. So was Maya after her divorce. Both succeeded brilliantly (though neither had to make her own living). Martha found her sense of purpose after she was diagnosed with her progressively debilitating disease, her husband left her, and she considered suicide; she decided she needed first to live for her daughter and then to help other people figure out how to turn seemingly insurmountable difficulties in their lives into opportunities.

After we've scribbled down our purpose, Martha asks us to write a few goals that will support that larger life purpose and make commitments to stick to them, i.e., spending more time writing and researching good stories. The results in our lives, she says, reveal what we're committed to. This makes uncomfortable sense to me: if I'd absolutely wanted children, I would have had them; when I really want to go to Italy, magically I find a way to get there. If being well off were important to me, I could've gone into business or law school or married one of the wealthy men who've crossed my path. I could have gotten married and settled down and had the companionship and stability I've been seeking, but I guess I didn't really want it that badly, not if it interfered with my bigger interest in traveling and writing. Still, I've spent the past five years with an ongoing writer's block, as if I've needed to settle some internal issues before I could turn my attention back out to the world.

If we want to change the results in our lives, Martha says, we have to change the beliefs that have led us to take specific actions and behaviors. Thinking it's impossible to be both independent and settle down means I have no partner, saying I can't afford a house means I have no permanent home; if I turned those assumptions around, things could turn out differently. Maybe.

I'm not sure how much I believe in this notion of manifesting your reality. At a certain point it can start sounding very New Age, like seminar leaders who convince you to spend your last thousand dollars learning about abundance. But Martha is more practical, and everything she says makes a certain amount of sense. Yet I can't get beyond agreeing intellectually with what she's writing on the flip charts to feeling and believing what she's putting forth. Nor can I get past the thought that sometimes shit happens, through no fault of your own.

Then Martha brings up the notion of accountability. We are

all at some level accountable for the events that happen in our lives, she says. We play a role and need to acknowledge that role in order to see how our participation affects how things end up. It's only when we see how our actions have everything to do with the results in our lives that we can start to change them.

Though this makes a certain amount of sense, I can't help thinking it's also a kind of thinking that is a luxury for people in the West, who can actually afford to make choices with their lives. When people are struggling to be free of trafficking or slavery, when their families have been murdered, when they are just doing their best to find enough food to survive, all that "you create your own reality" stuff isn't just wasted breath but a dangerous way to think. You can change your reaction to circumstances, but not always the circumstances themselves.

I pipe up that this line of thinking strikes me as pretty unsympathetic, sort of a "blame the victim" philosophy, but Martha insists that accountability is different from blame. Then she points out that I'm pretty resistant to the whole process and says, "Whatever you resist, persists." Without being judgmental, she seems to have sized me up, suggesting that I don't like rules or authority, I like to go off on my own, I'm a lot more sensitive than I seem, I joke to cover up my feelings, I operate out of a great deal of fear, and I'm a perfectionist, sometimes preferring not to do something than to risk failure. "Perfectionists never win," she says.

I'm wondering if someone has slipped her my astrology chart. Maybe I am just an obvious type. In any case, I decide to set aside my reservations about people in the Third World, and play along with the game, since I am someone who is indeed lucky enough to be able to make choices in her life.

Martha asks us to try an exercise with a partner in which we tell a story where we've been victimized. I realize I don't know where to start: I'm always telling those kinds of stories. Take the tales I recount about bad dates. In each, I am a fun-loving, out-doorsy gal who likes Alice Munro, African dance, organic veg-etables, *The Wire,* and anything Italian, who mysteriously ends up being the hapless bystander on a bad date, suffering in the com-pany of one of the many clueless, damaged, shallow, narcissistic single males over forty who populate our major coastal cities. But the Big Story, in which I'm the sorriest victim, is the tale of my divorce, betrayal, heartbreak, and subsequent financial ruin at the hands of my ex-husband.

What if, asks Martha, when we are all finished telling our stories, wiping sorry tears from our eyes, you told that story dif-ferently? What if you told it as if you were accountable for what happened? How did you end up in that situation? What was your part?

I'm reluctant, but I try it and mention the choices I made, the red flags I ignored, such as the rattling snake and the fact that I'd brushed aside my ex-husband's ambivalence because I was deter-mined to get married and have children. I tell the story that way, and surprisingly, it is a relief. Blame does not fall down upon my head.

I see I made mistakes, to be sure. "The great thing about mistakes is that if you recognize them, you don't have to repeat them," Martha says.

This is a liberating, reassuring thought: instead of being the unwitting victim in my marriage, apt to be victimized in any subsequent relationships, I simply don't have to marry that guy again. It's in my power to recognize my mistakes. Nor do I have to be afraid of a new relationship, constantly choosing inappropriate men to date so I'll have an excuse to avoid what has become my greatest fear: being vulnerable, giving my heart, and being hurt. Have I been dating viable partners, Martha asks, or finding yet another character in a story who would prove it was ridiculous for me to be in a relationship? It seems that I am going to have to fundamentally change my stories about men—even if they won't be so funny to tell my friends—if I want a different, happier ending.

I'm surprised at how happy I feel after retelling my story, a huge weight lifted from me. I'm no longer the victim of a bad marriage, destined to be hurt all over again with any man I am foolish enough to give my trust and heart to. I think of all the other victim-type stories I tell myself: it's impossible to buy a house as a single freelance writer, my generation of independent and feminist women is out of sync with men and so will inevitably end up single or unfulfilled, I can't lose weight because my parents put me on a diet at an early age, men my age are only interested in younger, thinner women, I can't write another book because it won't sell as well as my last one, I'm middle-aged and stuck, blah, blah, blah. I have to turn all that thinking around if I'm going to be happy here in midlife. All those stories need different endings—which is possible, because it's my life and I do have the privilege of being able to write the story.

I think about the story I can't tell out loud to the group, about Samoa. From the start, I blamed myself—I was foolish and drunk. Subsequently, I've been afraid to travel alone, though I've managed it a few times, yet always fearful that I will uncontrollably land in a similar situation, unable to trust myself. The damage seems permanent and even embedded in my body: whatever tendon or ligament pulled in my hip has never recovered, despite all manner of acupuncture, physical therapy, doctor's visits, and yoga. The unease feels permanent, too. But though I can account for my role in what happened—I did get drunk, I did unwisely go walking on the beach with a man I didn't know—I don't have to blame myself for what happened next. Blame seems to solidify the sense of permanent damage and powerlessness. I can, however, avoid drinking in a strange situation, and sit with my feelings instead of dulling them with alcohol. (It strikes me, in fact, that I could avoid a lot of uncomfortable situations in my life if I cut way down on drinking alcohol, which turns out to be true.) Next time, instead of getting trashed with some Samoan drag queens, I can rely on my good judgment and go back to my hut and read a book.

If I don't let myself be a victim in my stories but understand my role as the protagonist of my own life, I can get my power back and trust myself that I can, through my actions or attitude, make things turn out all right.

For the next several months, my colleagues from that seminar are on a tear, getting big book deals and important magazine assignments, falling in love and having babies. I did not expect to find magic in a woman in a corporate suit with a flip chart, but I'm happy she's waved her wand over us. It seems easier for my colleagues to make big changes, as it was for my fellow Outward Bounders, but maybe my progress is more internal. In any case, it's slower and more subtle, but as I write down some weekly goals and stick to them, I begin to feel something shift, something lurching ahead.

NOT LONG AFTER, a former diplomat contacts me via an Ivy League Internet site I forgot I signed up with to ask me out. We meet for drinks at one of my favorite restaurants, which turns into dinner, with a beautiful bottle of Pinot Noir and a wide-ranging conversation. This, I think, is exactly the kind of man I'd like to be with. He is tall, thoughtful, well versed in an astounding variety of international issues, and wears shiny shoes with bright blue laces.

At the end of the evening, he drops me off at my place, and I invite him in for a nightcap, since he is a gentleman and we're having such a good conversation. "Let's go to Buenos Aires," he says, finishing his last drink. "B.A. is such a sexy city. I've got time off in two weeks."

Ordinarily, I am the first person to sign up when an attractive, intelligent, Oxford-educated man mentions going to sexy Buenos Aires next week. After I give him a kiss on the cheek good night and wave him off in a cab, I get as far as pulling out my tango shoes and checking flights. Then I realize that as wonderful a man as he seems, one of those high-SAT guys I should've snagged in college, his wife left him recently, and he is heartbroken and looking for a quick fix to make it better. Here in middle age, after all that meditation, goal setting, and reflection on accountability, I understand that healing takes time, he is in for a bumpy ride, and it isn't going to be with me on the way to Argentina.

There would be no satisfying ending to that story, not right now, not for me, and, much as I hate to squelch a good adventure involving travel and romance, there's some compensation in knowing I'm taking care of myself. When he calls, I tell him how delighted I was to meet him and to have dinner with him, and I hope we can do it again sometime. And then we'll see how the story goes.

Chapter Thirteen

SAN MIGUEL DE ALLENDE, MEXICO

2007, WEEK ONE

In the middle of winter, an editor calls asking me to do a story about women in San Miguel de Allende, Mexico, expatriates who have reinvented themselves in that town, pursuing second acts in their careers after forty.

I haven't been back to San Miguel de Allende, a well-preserved colonial town in the middle of the country—if you were to twirl Mexico on your finger, the tip would be touching San Miguel—since I lived there for a summer when I was ten. In all the years and trips since, I've never considered returning, even though I've visited several other places in Mexico. I've been afraid the town would be as changed as my childhood home in Colorado, surrounded by housing developments that obscure the mountains, and teeming with traffic. I've heard the place is full of gringos—bohemians, boomer artists, energy healers, Texas real estate developers, and retirees who realize that all of San Miguel, with its relatively inexpensive maids and medical services, amounts to assisted living, with better food.

I haven't wanted to mar the memory of the town that so thor-

oughly enchanted me thirty-five years ago. That summer stands
out in Technicolor among the black-and-white snapshots of my
childhood. There's my oldest sister, Cindy, her toothy smile bright
as the armful of sunflowers she bought for only a few pesos at
the market. That's Jan, with her long blond hair, trailed around
the central plaza by an amorous *muchacho* in a yellow VW bug.
There are Amy and me, skipping over cobblestones in our new
leather huaraches, on the way to the blue-doored bakery in the
morning to buy pastries in all different shapes that all tasted the
same. Here we are in Spanish class with our tiny teacher, whose
black braids reached to her knees and doubled back again, pinned
behind her ears. Dad's patting a donkey in that shot. And there's
Mom, sunning her legs in the open courtyard where we lived, her
face shaded by the flowering plants that spilled over the wooden
balcony.

Yet San Miguel de Allende still tugs at my subconscious.
I've always been curious about the town, reading about it from
afar, hearing reports from friends who have wandered through.
I am curious enough to agree to the assignment; in any case, it's
my job.

I ARRIVE VERY late in León and take a shuttle van, an hour and
a half, to San Miguel de Allende. The high desert is empty of
all but scraggly brush, the distant hills barely visible in the night,
stars sprinkling the sky like salt. I sink back into my brain and
try to come up with enough Spanish to make polite conversation
with the driver, the basics about where he lives and how many

kids he has. Younger than me, with five children, he is already a grandfather a few times over.

Because I'm tired and don't want to try to explain about being single and childless to a man from a culture where that doesn't make sense, I tell the driver a story when he asks, that I have a son, Antonio, who is studying Spanish for a summer at the University of Guanajuato before he goes to college. I'm in Mexico to visit him and spend a few days in San Miguel with some old friends, I say. My husband—who, *gracias a Dios,* is still as handsome as the day we married, at least I think so—had to stay at home because he is a transplant specialist and has to be on call in case someone dies in an accident and he has to rush to harvest the organs. In my Spanish it comes out sounding more like "he specializes in people's organ meats and has to be ready to run and cut out the fresh heart and brains."

"Ah." The driver nods gravely, ready to switch topics.

As we pass vast expanses of brush, limbs reaching to the desert moon, I ask the driver what I fear most about San Miguel de Allende, that under the stress of time and development, with the influx of artists and Texans, it has been ruined. I want to be prepared. He tells me that there are indeed more and more gringos and more development, and that many Mexicans who grew up there are taking the crazy money they made from selling their little houses in town and moving somewhere bigger, but not necessarily better, farther out.

It's good and bad, he says.

There's money and there's work, but what's the point if you can't live where you grew up, where it's the most beautiful, *lo más bonito.* He sighs. "You get a little older, and everything always changes," he says.

"*Así es la vida,*" I say. I'm considering turning back around, but it's one in the morning and we're nearly there.

"*Así es.*"

A little later, coming into view of the reservoir outside of town, the driver asks if I've been to San Miguel de Allende before, and I say I lived here for a while, as a child. I can tell that gives me a little credibility; I haven't just read about the place in *Sunset* magazine and decided to come down to build a big dream house. "*Fue muy mágico,*" I tell him.

It had indeed been magical. In 1971, Mom got the idea to take us four daughters to Mexico for the summer. This was before her Outward Bound trip, but she was already on her adventure streak. She wanted us to see something of the world outside Littleton, a suburb where most dads worked for aerospace companies and almost everyone voted Republican.

But Mom could venture only so far outside Littleton. Since we weren't going to move out of the suburbs—Dad, a pediatrician, had an established practice in town, and they both enjoyed the sprawling lawn and proximity to the mountains—she brought other cultures into our home. Or, as we kids saw it, she brought home strays. Every few months, new people would take up residence in the guest room: Navajo children, a Cuban family, Swiss exchange students, visiting Greeks. During the Vietnam War, she opened the door to several antiwar students who were participating in a program called "ATSIV," which is "VISTA" spelled backward, in which instead of going into poor neighborhoods to work, postcollege kids went into wealthier homes to "raise the consciousness" of the suburbs and to have a nice free place to stay and meals to eat between demonstrations. June, my favorite of these ATSIV students, splashed around naked in a fountain in downtown Denver just to see what would happen (she got arrested, then eventually went on to drive a cab, join a cult, adopt a guru-bestowed name, and settle in a communal house in northern California with both her boyfriend and her ex-husband, practicing visualization and taking esoteric workshops in self-improvement).

My father wasn't exactly thrilled with this parade of visitors, though he'd go along with the invasions cheerfully enough as long as he could occasionally shut the door to his den, light a pipe, and read in peace. Dad sometimes lost his affable composure when a hippie student crashed his motorcycle trying to put it in reverse or played Frank Zappa really loud when he came home from seeing wailing babies and fretting mothers all day long, and then he'd decide his consciousness had been raised quite enough. He was more interested in the foreign students than the political ones and eager to inflict his Spanish, French, or German on whomever was passing through. Now and then he went off to work on a reservation with the Native American public health services and is proud to say he's the only white guy you'll ever meet who can do a complete physical in Navajo.

When Mom brought up the idea of moving to Mexico for the summer, Dad was initially reluctant. It's not as if you could trust the hippie students to mow the lawn in perfectly even stripes, the way he does. But as with most things—voting Democrat, getting a toy poodle, hosting radical prison activists for cocktails—he eventually went along with Mom's idea. She'd heard about San Miguel de Allende from her friend Janet MacKenzie, another of the dozen Democrats in Littleton, whose artistic and worldly tastes far transcended the avocado green, shag-rug ambience of the neighborhood. Jan MacKenzie had recently returned from several weeks in San Miguel de Allende, tanned and resplendent in colorful woven shawls and oversized pieces of silver jewelry, her four children effortlessly chattering in Spanish. The MacKenzies had studied at an art school, the Instituto Allende, and stayed at a boardinghouse in the center of town.

Mom started planning our trip.

The art scene is what made San Miguel de Allende a magnet for the Jan MacKenzies of the world. An American-accredited fine arts school, the Escuela Universitaria de Bellas Artes, opened in 1938, and by 1948, several former World War II soldiers on the G.I. Bill discovered that they could attend school and live very well in San Miguel on their modest grants. That year, *Life* magazine ran a three-page spread on the place. "GI Paradise: Veterans Go to Mexico to Study Art, Live Cheaply and Have a Good Time," reporting that apartments were $10 a month, full-time maids another $8, and rum 65 cents a quart. The resulting influx of would-be painters, sculptors, jewelry makers, and rummies spurred the opening of another accredited art school, the Instituto Allende, in 1950. By the 1960s, San Miguel de Allende was a counterculture destination for U.S. truth seekers and acidheads, including Ken Kesey; they came down off their high in 1968 when the notorious beatnik Neal Cassady, woozy on barbiturates after a wedding in San Miguel, wandered back along the train tracks to Celaya, apparently to count them, wearing only a T-shirt and jeans on a cold and rainy night, and was found in a coma the next day, dying in a nearby hospital just short of his forty-second birthday. Still, many of the artists and expats stayed on, forever painting the pink facade of the Gothic La Parroquia church in the main square, seeking spiritual enlightenment, and creating a community that welcomed other like-minded bohemians. They opened galleries and coffee shops, an English library, and, inevitably, real estate offices. By the 1970s, it had calmed down enough to become a popular place for artsy and progressive parents to bring their kids for a summer to safely introduce them to another culture.

And so we set off for Mexico by bus from El Paso. This was our second time in that country: we'd gone to Baja a few years before, but all I remember, besides the vast novelty of the ocean, was how mortified my nearly teenaged sisters were when I rolled down the window and yelled "¿*CÓMO ESTÁ USTED?*" as loudly as I could to the first Mexican I saw, who politely waved back.

The bus was cramped and dusty, but I was too interested in how everything changed, once in Mexico, to care. The guy at the border checks your passports, waves you through, and, just like that, people speak a different language, dress in clothes that don't match, and sell seeds you crack and scatter the shells of on the floor of the bus. You had to pay to use the bathroom at the stops, and it was someone's job to sit there, collect the pesos, and hand you three squares of something that was closer to wrapping paper than tissue. The arid landscape was the same as in Texas, as were the cowboy hats and pickup trucks, but other than that, every-thing in Mexico was instantly different.

When we reached Mexico City we had wilted, and it may
be that some of us were whining. We waited and waited for another bus that didn't come as scheduled, and when it finally arrived, the bus to San Miguel de Allende made the one from El
Paso seem outrageously luxurious. It had school bus–style bench
seats, springs sproinging out of thin green vinyl, people sitting
precariously on laps and standing in the aisles, and crates of live
chickens aboard. With no shocks, the bus jolted us out of sleepi-
ness with every winding, lurching turn. Outside Mexico City we
saw miles of slums, poverty that television only hinted at or on the
news—a long way from Littleton.

Then the desert landscape was the same for hours, slowly ris-
ing, and we were almost managing sleep when we rounded a corner and came upon a Mexican Oz: a city of sunset-colored houses
sloping down to a central pink spire.

The bus let us out in the center of town, near another church
and a square. We suddenly felt very gringo, surrounded by our
suitcases, probably more stuff than the people around us owned.
We ate steaming tacos with our hands and drank orange sodas.
Then we were able to take in the town the trees dripping with
flowers, the old cheek-to-cheek buildings that would have been
plain-faced but for their marvelous colors: pink, crab apple, mari-
gold, Fanta orange. The streets weren't paved, exactly, but covered in flat, irregular stones, like an old, smooth riverbed. After
the dreary bus ride, suddenly everything seemed calm and colorful, infused with waning shades of sunlight. We piled ourselves
into a couple of taxis that threaded through narrow, one-way
streets on the way to our new, temporary home.

We passed donkeys, indignant under their heavy loads. We

drove by houses where the tops of the walls were embedded with glass shards to keep burglars out (though a cat was delicately making its path across the broken bottles, undisturbed). Finally we pulled up to a stucco house with a heavy carved wooden door. The place seemed stark and forbidding, with no wide screen doors, lawns, sprinklers, or anything else we associated with summer. We girls glanced at one another nervously: we were going to spend our precious summer *here*?

And then someone opened the door. Inside was a world of green, of flowers, birdcages, fountains, and painted tile floors. A magic garden. The house seemed to be mostly outdoor space, with the rooms surrounding the courtyard almost an afterthought. The proprietress, a stout woman with curly gray hair and woven, ethnic-looking clothes, bustled about, showing us to our simple whitewashed rooms with twin wooden beds, each with a cross above the headboard. Amy and I flopped down, the fan cooling our humid skin, taking us into a slumber of tropical dreams and anticipation.

In the morning, I woke to the sound of bells and roosters and a maid swishing her broom on the tiles. Mexico! I nudged Amy, who gave me a sleepy grin, and pushed her harder because it was morning and we were in Mexico and there was no time to spare. We got out of bed, feet cold on the tiled floor, and peeked out the window. In the courtyard, the sun was just touching the lush tropical plants, lighting the pink flowers, shining the surface of the water in the stone fountain. The other doors around the patio were closed. We made our way, shyly, to a breakfast of crusty bolillo rolls with marmalade. "*Gracias,*" I said to the maid, who smiled—Spanish words actually *work*—and I was eager to go outside, to explore the town, to learn new words, to make all that was strange familiar.

WITH THESE MEMORIES swirling around in my head, anticipating my return to San Miguel with both eagerness and dread, we finally come into view of the town. The lights are so widespread it seems as if San Miguel de Allende has spent the past thirty-five years outgrowing itself, sprawling away from its colonial streets. On the edges of town, identical condos line up behind locked gates like prisoners waiting for the count and housing developments march up into the foothills and scatter. My heart sinks as we enter town, when we pass a fast-food chicken restaurant and a supersized grocery store. "That's new," says the driver.

I wonder if the *mercado,* where short, gnarled women pressed still-warm tortillas into our hands, still exists.

Nothing about this San Miguel de Allende seems familiar, until we turn a corner onto a narrow, crooked street, our way lit by wrought-iron lampposts that cast rosy circles of glow. I don't know where I am, but I have been here before. We stop in front of the hotel, and the driver leaves. I give the night attendant my name and he checks the book; there is no reservation for me tonight. Maybe I am so late that my room has been given away, another sign that I shouldn't even be here. The night man is baffled about what to do. I ask if there is a room, any room, and he nods. Phew. The rate? He is perplexed again.

"*Mañana,*" I say. We'll figure it out tomorrow.

He smiles broadly and picks up my bag. *"Mañana."*

He leads me through a garden, with tiled stairways curving up to balconied rooms. It is January, and poinsettias are everywhere in pots. My room has an arched doorway and white stucco walls; the bathroom is covered in uneven blue and yellow tiles. The carved bed is firm, with white linens, and, exhausted after a long journey, I fall right in.

But I'm excited and can't sleep. In some ways, I am coming back to where I started, as a traveler at least, and I have a sense of summing up, like you have right before your birthday, or on New Year's Eve after a few too many drinks, when you wonder what you did with all that time. Part of me fears that if I walk around San Miguel, I might come face-to-face with the ten-year-old I used to be, and I would disappoint her. What would that bright pigtailed girl, who roamed freely around San Miguel, a whole new world of experience and language opening up to her, so eager to come home and write stories about it for her sixth-grade class, think about her forty-five-year-old self?

She would've been thrilled to know that one day she would indeed travel to many countries and be awed by so many sights, tastes, and people, but otherwise she might've been confused by the reality of herself at middle age: no husband, kids, or house, not even an international affair with some mysterious Basil St. John with his dark eye patch and orchid serum, like Brenda Starr. Not right now, anyway. I toss in bed, wrestling with my ten-year-old self.

And then I am woken by bells and by blue light streaming through the corner of the wood-framed window. And just like that ten-year-old, I jump out of bed.

*   *   *

THAT FIRST MORNING it's chilly, the high-altitude air holding no heat, tiles cold to the bare feet. I'm eager to leave the hotel and walk around town. In the morning light, the buildings are as colorful as in my memory, but they all seem to be in the wrong places. Everything I see is like looking at a painting where the artist has taken familiar objects out of context in order to make them unfamiliar, so that you can see them anew.

I make my way around San Miguel's crooked corners for several hours, wandering by instinct and deep memory. I find the park nearby, with its crisscrossing trails, sun streaming through overhanging trees, amateur paintings for sale. The faces of the Spanish-style houses, dating back as far as the seventeenth century, haven't changed their expressions. I pass the blue-doored bakery, where people have loaded up trays with pastries since 1910, children tugging on their parents' sleeves to add some more. Street vendors roast ears of corn and sell tidy piles of fresh handmade tortillas. A languid perfume drifts in the air, and in the town's shady *jardín,* tourists and residents sit on the benches, eating chunks of cool watermelon, watching children run to the balloon sellers, and staring up at the towering pink La Parroquia church.

Other things I encounter in San Miguel seem jarringly new and out of place. I barely recognize the boardinghouse where we stayed when I was ten. Its facade has been modernized, and behind its walls are a bank, a gallery, a jewelry store, and a hotel that is under renovation, probably for the third time since we were there; there are no more turkeys on the roof. (It is hard to imagine that my mother left me and my sister Amy here alone for five days, at ages ten and twelve, with only a housekeeper, while she went off to Pátzcuaro with my older sisters, but it didn't faze us one bit to roam the streets by ourselves.) Now there's too much traffic for children to play; SUVs clog the streets where there used to be only burros and VW bugs. There are many more gringos, fewer beggars, tourists everywhere, boutiques, chic restaurants, and talk of a Starbucks café on the main square. Good and bad, as the taxi driver said.

I BECOME REACQUAINTED with the town, and though it has indeed changed since I was ten, so has the whole world, and San Miguel has managed to retain its rustic, artsy, small-town charm. The town slowly reveals itself to me and surprises me, like the Spanish that has been lying dormant in my brain for so many years, which suddenly surfaces, as if being where I learned the language in the first place brings it all back. The atmosphere in San Miguel is slow and pleasant, as if they put lithium into the bottled water, but there is plenty to do. I explore the cactus collection and the trails hugging the canyon at the botanical gardens. I swim in the hot springs pool outside town—the place that lured people to settle here centuries ago, where I remember wondering, as a child, why the other kids wore their underwear instead of bathing suits. I make chiles en nogales at a cooking school in the country and read at a book club. I wander around innumerable art galleries and jewelry stores, which are quite democratic, in that it seems that anyone who has decided, after all these years, to try his or her hand at painting or silversmithing can exhibit his or her wares alongside those of a few real masters. And almost every night I dance—at parties, at clubs, and at salsa lessons, where, by the end of the evening, several drunken Mexican men half my age are begging to come home with me. I smooch a sexy Mexican musician after a jazz concert before I find out that he (like most seemingly available Latin men in their forties or fifties, especially musicians) is married.

Right away, I find that it's easy to meet people here, especially women over forty, who are given to loose cotton tunics, stunning big jewelry, and heavy-soled shoes that are comfortable on the cobblestones. Perhaps because they've found other, mainly single women in like circumstances, the women in San Miguel are very social: you can walk outside your door, meet someone on the side-walk for the first time, and get invited over.

On one of my first mornings I go to a yoga class and meet up with Paige, a fifty-year-old with spiky red hair, the only person I know from San Francisco. She meets me in the sunflower yel-low Bellas Artes building, where you enter an enormous wooden door into the former convent courtyard and cross into a mirrored dance studio. The students, many well into their retired years, are amiable, cheerfully shifting their mats over to make room—not like in a crowded class in San Francisco or New York, where a yogini pretending to be meditating on the beauty of now is in-wardly cursing the bitch four inches to the right who arrived late and is intruding on her space.

After class, Paige and I sit in a café on the jardín, under bloodred arches, the sun warming us as we shed early-morning layers. She tells me she came here with her partner on vacation

and ended up deciding to return, partly because they met so many
interesting women who are escapees from their previous lives,
pursuing new paths.

"You run into so many women here who are divorced, widows, retired—and all of them are blooming," Paige says. People
fall in love with the place, she says, particularly given the favorable economics of living south of the border in a town with excellent gringo infrastructure (wireless Internet, English bookstores,
organic vegetables, U.S. mailboxes). She and her partner took a
bold step, giving up San Francisco altogether for Mexico. They
sold their house, packed up their stuff, and are using the spoils
of San Francisco's real estate boom to stop working full-time and
build the home they always dreamed of in the Mexican countryside. They'll write, they'll paint, they'll figure out their next steps
later on. Paige is animated, full of all the energy she says drained
out of her in the past few years in San Francisco, working all the
time, stuck in a harried routine to pay a bloated mortgage.

For now, she and her partner are living in a house they built
last year, a temporary place while their house in the country is
being built. We walk back to Guadalupe, their flat *colonia,* or
neighborhood, just outside the historic center. Paige's blood-
orange casa has three bedrooms, a garage, a spacious kitchen,
and a rooftop terrace—much larger than where they lived in San
Francisco.

"Not that it was easy," said Paige. She pulls out photos of a
grease-spattered hovel, which they bought for $75,000, a fortune
to the owners. I wouldn't have had the imagination to look at that
wreck and see a lovely adobe house with cathedral ceilings and

a big tiled kitchen. Paige's story of buying her lot, designing the house, and having it built sounds like an exciting, creative adventure—for them. For me, it would be a hassle, a logistical nightmare, and a money pit. At the very least, it strikes me that for such a project you'd need a partner to check the plans, do the math on the mortgage, help you settle on the kitchen counters, and figure out where to put the powder room. Just getting the necessary permits, paying a lot of fees, and standing in lines, Paige says, tested the limits of even the most patient American yogini. Nothing was ever done correctly the first time; they built the walls first and then tore them up to add the electricity later on. Everything took longer and cost more than expected. They had to keep an eye on the construction every step of the way. Communication problems translated into expensive mistakes. In other words, all the typical headaches of renovation in the United States times ten.

Yet the idea of building a house makes me wistful. How much fun to choose which room is best for a study, figure out how you'd like the kitchen to flow into the dining room, pick out cheerful tiles for the kitchen. How wonderful to have a place in the world you could call your own, where you could be at home but, in a foreign culture with a new language, still feel as though you were traveling.

The fantasy of buying real estate in San Miguel intrigues me enough that I decide to look around, just for fun. I don't know why—I haven't the faintest idea what I could afford, if anything, but looking at real estate almost seems like a ritual when you visit the town, like checking out the inside of the big pink La Parroquia church or buying a fringed shawl you'll never wear at home.

In the cafés around the jardín in San Miguel, everyone seems to be discussing real estate. Some are on cell phones making deals, and many of the artists talking about painting are actually referring to the colors of their walls. Walking around the historic *centro,* real estate office windows are papered with photos of colonial houses and Santa Fe–style condos, all with price tags approaching those of San Francisco.

I go see a Realtor named Manuel, on a lark, and when I take a wild guess at my price range, his face falls, the way a professional matchmaker's did a few months earlier when I visited her downtown office in San Francisco and told her I was looking for a smart, single, relatively undamaged man around my own age to date. There just isn't much out there for me.

Still, Manuel does his best and shows me a few lots in the far-flung colonias of San Miguel de Allende that I could afford. These are neighborhoods where the gringo cafés haven't yet reached, where you would need to take a bus or a taxi to get to the center of town. One place way up a hill has a great view, and though it is easy to fantasize building a house with a sweeping vista and an attached studio or guest space, it is much harder to imagine walking back from the market every day lugging a woven plastic bag full of groceries.

So I've done my research. Obviously, San Miguel de Allende—like San Francisco—is out of my price range. If I want to live in the outskirts, maybe I could afford something, but I'm single and like to live where there are other people nearby and I can get around by walking. In San Miguel, that's the historic center.

"*Algo en el centro?*" I asked Manuel.

He rolled his eyes. "*Nada.*"

So that's that. But as I have a beer near the jardín as evening falls, I am reluctant to give up the fantasy. I feel an attachment to this town I visited thirty-five years ago, and to this jardín, where young men and women came out for the paseo in the evening, a parade of public courting, stealing glances at one another under the watchful eyes of their relatives, holding hands if they were going to be engaged. Now people walk every which way, the couples make out in dim doorways, but there are still music, fireworks, mariachis, dancing, and friends who run into each other and greet each other with kisses.

Chapter Fourteen

SAN MIGUEL DE ALLENDE

2007, Week Two

For a week, I've been lulled into dreaminess in San Miguel, and this morning I have to be alert. First, I need to find a new place to stay. After house-sitting for a few days, I spent last night in a garden room in a fabulous colonial house full of sumptuous plants, parrot cages, and bohemian objets d'art, presided over by a woman of fearless style. Unfortunately, the place smells strongly of the macaque monkeys that also reside there. I woke up with a sickly sweet ammonia smell clinging to my hair and need to move.

That's not all I have to figure out this morning: the story I came to report was supposed to be about a business two women started here, but it has gradually dawned on me that the enterprise barely exists beyond a press release, the two women aren't speaking to each other, and no one is giving me a straight story because both of them want to be featured in a national magazine article anyway. I have to round up someone else to profile, fast, someone who made a sea change in her life at forty and started a business in San Miguel, and then make the case to my meticulously cautious editor for a switcheroo before the photographers show up tomorrow.

Wandering around the neighborhood, I run across an unmarked garage door with a small metal hot-air balloon hanging above. I've heard it's the studio of a local jewelry company, so I knock. A chic young Mexican woman in jeans and layers of long necklaces opens the door. Inside the workshop, images of the Virgin of Guadalupe and other icons cover the walls, carved wooden altars perch on desks, and sparkling crystals and jewelry are strewn about the tables. I'm curious about this little world, which has a strong, spirited, feminine vibe.

The young woman introduces me to Cheryl, the owner and designer, who looks about my age, with smart-girl glasses, a warm smile, and a black rose tattoo. Right away she invites me to sit down and have some dark chocolate with her, asks what I'm doing in San Miguel, and tells me the story of how she ended up in San Miguel, leaving her executive husband and job in fashion marketing in San Francisco to go to a yoga retreat. She stayed on, first selling falafel and hummus to get by, then making funky little bags with Virgin of Guadalupe fobs, evolving to crystal-encrusted necklaces and belt buckles based on Mexican folklore and goddess iconography. Judging from the photos tacked up of celebrities wearing her designs, she has done very well.

Cheryl fingers an ornate rosary-looking necklace she designed. "I'm not a practicing Catholic, but I love mythology," she says. "These icons are calming and feminine and ancient. I like to think they carry a little magic."

She asks where I'm staying, and I tell her I need a place. She

calls her friend Delphine, who has a room down the street, problem solved. I also need a new subject for my article and realize
she's sitting in front of me. *Perfecto.* Cheryl writes down names of
other women who might be appropriate for the piece and tells me
to call so we can hang out later on.

She gives me a kiss on the cheek as I leave. "My friends call
me Finn."

"Finn."

DELPHINE'S HOUSE IS just a few doors away, across from
the bullring. I knock, and, as with so many doors in San Miguel
de Allende, hers opens onto a surprisingly large, sunny central
courtyard. A thin, elegant man greets me, explains that Delphine
stepped out; he is a tango teacher who is staying here, holding
classes in a studio out back. I'm glad I packed my dancing shoes.

Then Roberto, who lives with Delphine, comes over and introduces himself, and we chat. Roberto is a salsa teacher who also
works in real estate. I say I'm thinking about taking salsa lessons,
and he tells me when classes are held. Then, for the sake of conversation, waiting there, I also say I've also considered building or
buying a house in San Miguel de Allende, but everything in the
centro seems unaffordable.

Roberto snaps his fingers. "I think I know a little place you
could look at."

I don't really feel like going to look at more real estate I can't
afford. That particular fantasy has passed. On the other hand, I
am just sitting here with my bag, waiting. "When?" I ask.

"How about now?"

Roberto maneuvers his Jeep up onto a small sidewalk on Calle Loreto, just a few blocks from the central square in San Miguel de Allende, on the less gringo side of town. He parks next to a lamppost, leaving just enough space for another car to pass if it folds in its side-view mirrors. "This is it," he says.

We're in front of a narrow, crumbling, two-story white building, its blue shutters bleached and battered from decades of sun and torrential afternoon rains. The house, squeezed into a row of other tall, thin houses, isn't quite as wide as a one-car garage. A turquoise band runs around the base of the building like the cuff of a frayed dress shirt, and an iron street lamp hangs from the facade by its ancient appendage. The house has a decrepit charm; the tourists passing by might take an artsy photo of it as a study in textured, colorful Mexican decay.

Roberto unlocks the sturdy mesquite door, and we step inside a brick-and-concrete shell with a drooping ceiling, old bills and plastic bags scattered on the floor. It smells dank and musty, the only recent visitors stray animals, probably including scorpions. Behind a flaking back door are the ruins of a staircase, a broken toilet and washbasin, pieces of corrugated iron where a roof should be, and a pile of refuse. I quickly head back out to the street.

"Well," I say.

"I think they'd take a hundred thousand dollars," Roberto says.

"Huh."

Getting into the Jeep, Roberto asks what I think of the place.

He says that even though it's tiny—three and a half meters wide by fourteen long—it has potential. All Realtors think every rundown place for sale has potential, but even he doesn't sound convinced.

"It's . . . small."

I don't know what else to say or even why I'm here, except that somehow, today, I have ended up standing in front of this little house in San Miguel's historic centro. Some days are like that when you're traveling: you follow your nose, and you never know where you'll end up. Roberto mentions that the restaurant a few doors down, the one with the iron bull outside, makes the best margaritas and fajitas in town. Scruffy boys kick soccer balls around on the gray cobblestones, dodging cars, while their mothers watch from windows behind ornate iron bars. Here in the middle of town, in the middle of the day, roosters crow, dogs bark, and a man in a tattered vest carries his knife-sharpening wheel, blowing a singsong whistle.

Just up the street is the artisan market. More than thirty-five years ago, my sister Amy and I used to love to wend our way to this mercado after Spanish class, to marvel at the endless stalls of hand-made treasures—onyx donkeys, tin stars, embroidered blouses, painted armadillos, mustachioed marionettes. We took a few of them home and put them on our windowsills to remind us of that sparkling market and that summer when we were free to roam the streets of a foreign country and practice a few new words of Spanish. I've never thrown away those little onyx donkeys.

Here on Calle Loreto is the sad, tiny turquoise-and-white house with its hand-painted FOR SALE sign, as neglected as one of the friendly stray mutts people adopt around town.

"I've seen enough," I tell Roberto.

He shrugs, adjusts his camouflage hat, and puts the car in gear. "I'll take it."

ROBERTO PULLS OUT his cell phone, calls the owner of the turquoise house, and, just like that, makes the offer.

I'm shocked that I said I'd buy the house, the words flying out of my mouth, propelled by some internal gremlin, bypassing my brain. It was an unexpected, irrational impulse, but it nevertheless hit me as the obvious, right thing to do, like knocking on Finn's door or renting a room at Delphine's. Maybe I'm being wildly impulsive. But I recall, when I first started meditating, that Sharon told me that I could prize my quickness and adventurous spirit if I could sort out my reactions from my deeper, intuitive responses. And as crazy as this decision seems, I somehow also feel that it's been brewing deep in my brain for some time.

"Wait," I urge Roberto as he's speaking. I do realize there is a whole string of considerations people weigh, carefully, before deciding to spend their entire freelance-writer life savings on 525 square feet in Mexico. It's not like buying boots. One ought to ask a few questions.

He puts his hand over the phone. "What?"

"Do you think I can get it for less?" I say. That's all I've come up with. I could probably use my sister Jan here now; she spent her entire summer in Mexico learning how to bargain in the market and has been bargaining ever since.

"No," he replies. "There's another offer on the house, so that's as low as they'll go."

"*Así es,*" I say. That's how it is.

"*Así es,*" he says, resuming the conversation. He closes his cell phone, and they have accepted my offer. I realize I don't even have a check for the down payment, but Roberto says he'll front the money until Friday, and in the meantime I can retrieve the maximum out of the ATM every day.

WE RETURN TO Delphine's house, where I meet her, a lean woman of indeterminate age with a white-blond ponytail, leggings, ankle boots, and a black hat. She's a painter, and the house is full of tall paintings, mainly of tango dancers. I notice how people seem to make their dreams come true in this town, like the way she has a tango studio in the back of her house where masters from around the world come to teach her *ocho cortados*. When I tell her I've just made an offer on a house, she is as enthusiastic as Roberto is blasé and as I am numbly full of wonder.

"That's what happens," she says. "People come down here and fall in love with the place, and pretty soon they're making an offer on a house."

Delphine shows me to my room, a simple and lovely whitewashed bedroom with cobalt blue tiles and dark Spanish wood furnishings. I splash water on my face and flop down on the bed. This room, I think, isn't any wider than eleven and a half feet. Well, maybe a little wider. I'm not really a very good judge of space.

Sitting there in the little white bedroom, daylight fading, I can't fathom that I've just decided, randomly, to buy a house. It hits me that as sure a decision as it seemed at the moment—if you can even call such an impulsive move a "decision"—there are a million reasons buying a tiny ruin in Mexico is foolish. I can't even begin the list.

I can't call my parents, sisters, or friends to talk it over, either, because they'll tell me I'm completely loco to even consider spending my entire life savings on an abandoned lot in Mexico that is only eleven and a half feet wide. They'll ask a lot of annoying questions, such as How are you going to design a house on such a small lot? Where will you live while construction is going on? How will you oversee building from San Francisco? What about all the permits? Where will you get the money to build? Who will rent it? Who will take care of it when you're not there? What about gas, electricity, and running water? and What happens if there's a revolution?

I get up from the bed and pace around the little room. I could still back out of the Mexico house. I haven't put any money down. I'm under no obligation. I could just say oops, sorry, my mistake, *disculpame,* let the other guy who supposedly had an offer on the place buy the house. Roberto would be pissed off, but getting pissed off at deals falling through is what happens to people who sell real estate. I'll be leaving town soon anyway, and already I've pretty much seen and done what there is to see and do here. I have a real affection for San Miguel de Allende, but so what—there are so many places left in the world to explore.

Yet I feel strangely settled about buying the house. Was it, as Delphine said, that I had come to San Miguel de Allende and fallen in love with the place? But I fall in love with places all the time and have never considered buying a home—except in San Francisco, where a divorce and a dot-com boom, ancient history by now, priced me out of the market. Or in Italy—which I've known as intimately as a lover, the wonderful and the infuriating, and where I've learned the language well enough that Italians don't always recognize me as American. But buying a little place of my own on my favorite Sicilian island has always been a fantasy too far out of reach, something I felt I could never do alone, and here in my forties, I am alone.

So why Mexico? I could say Mexico is the new Italy, now that the dollar can be used as toilet paper in Europe. Mexico, too, is full of gorgeous buildings and piazzas, rich history and art and remarkable cuisines. But really, Mexico is Mexico.

Then is it like settling for second best just because I'm in my forties and it's getting late? Instead of the smart, funny, good-looking guy who is well read and easygoing and heads outdoors whenever he can—an entrepreneur who loves Nabokov, Scrabble, Barolo, and bicycling over the Golden Gate Bridge, say—I'm going for the guy I'm not wildly in love with but who is okay, maybe the best I can get here in middle age, me with my extra fifteen pounds and countless imperfections and tendencies toward . . . impulsiveness? So if I can't have Italy, I'll settle for Mexico?

No: whatever drove that crazy decision to buy the house, it wasn't resignation. It may be fate, magic, or stupidity, but the only person I seem to be listening to is the ten-year-old in me, who is thrilled with the idea of buying a little house in San Miguel, right near the mercado.

*   *   *

THE NEXT MORNING, after draining the ATM for the day, I have to tell someone what I've done. I start with Sandra, who will be easy. She is enthusiastic in general and loves Mexico in particular; since she lived next door to me in San Francisco for years, she understands that I can never afford to buy a place there but would like to own something, somewhere. She's photographed textiles in Chiapas and the Day of the Dead in Pátzcuaro, and now says she can't wait to visit San Miguel. "Fantastic," she says.

Buoyed, I call my sister Cindy.

"Wow," she says, surprised. "It was such an impulsive move. Did you get any sleep last night?"

"Of course," I say. "I have plenty of experience being impulsive."

Cindy laughs. I can almost hear her shaking her head, marveling at what crazy thing I've done now. She's used to me calling and saying I'm off to Vietnam on a bicycling trip or need to go to Argentina next week. Then, more seriously: "Have you thought it through? Do you think it'll be a good investment?"

"Definitely," I say, even though when it comes to the math, permits, or construction, I haven't actually thought it through at all. I made this decision on intuition, and I'm assuming it'll eventually work out. I don't really want to think about it in terms of an investment.

"It's a great investment," I say and come up with some reasons for why that could be true: it'll be easy to rent, since it's walkable to everything, and the historic centro, including my little lot, is about to be declared a UNESCO World Heritage Site. If there's one thing I've learned from living in San Francisco, it's that in an architecturally charming, culturally savvy city with no room to grow, sooner or later real estate is bound to go up. San Francisco is out of my price range, but the smallest house in San Miguel is not.

"So how small is small?" Cindy asks.

I hesitate before answering, because it sounds so ridiculous. "About eleven and a half feet wide."

"Huh," she says. Concerned.

"It'll be cute," I say. I'm not worried about living in a really small house. New Yorkers live in small spaces all the time. The narrowest house in Greenwich Village—a converted alley where Edna St. Vincent Millay lived—is only 9.5 feet wide, so at 11.5 feet wide, this place is positively spacious.

"Well," says Cindy, "how much space do you really need, anyway?"

"Right," I say. Cindy and her family live in a little house on a big piece of land and, like me, believe in small spaces and minimal living for environmental reasons and also because it forces you not to accumulate too much stuff, which is an American disease. I see friends who have garages and spare rooms packed with big plastic Tupperware-like boxes and am glad I'm limited to two hall closets and the space beneath my bed. Having less stuff makes me feel light. I'm definitely guilty of having too many books and shoes, but we're all guilty of something.

"Sounds like an adventure, anyway," says Cindy, and then she asks where the house is, to see if she can place it from her memory of the town.

"Right near the mercado," I tell her.

"Oh," says Cindy, and her voice becomes dreamy. "I remember getting huge bouquets of sunflowers there for only a few pesos."

"You still can."

THE ONLY OTHER person I tell about buying the house is Finn, whom I run into at a café with her little daughter, Tallulah, who is dressed in pink with sparkly shoes.

"You won't believe it," I say. "I made an offer on a house."

"Honey!" Finn says, thrilled. "That's great!" She wants to hear the whole story, so I tell it, including the part about the irresistible, inexplicable impulse to buy the house.

"It was meant to be," Finn says with such certainty that I'm feeling a little less crazy—or maybe a little more New Agey.

She insists we walk down to Calle Loreto to see the property.

"This is it," I say, a few minutes later, standing in front of the house. It suddenly looks a lot narrower than I thought. "It's tiny," I say, back to feeling extremely uncertain. Really, it's a complete dump.

"It's adorable!" Finn says, then asks Tallulah what she thinks. She considers it. "The fairies can play here," she says.

We make our way back, past the mercado toward the jardín. "It's a great location," says Finn. "That house is a little gold mine."

A GOLD MINE. I've been sitting in the attorney's fusty office for the past forty-five minutes with the owners of the turquoise house, ready to sign the papers, but at the last moment, the elderly

señora is refusing to sell. From what I gather, she thinks there's
treasure buried on the property—silver, and maybe gold.

The diminutive woman, in her dark blue shawl, checkered
pinafore skirt, and weathered Indian face, is squabbling with her
well-pressed son, who is brushing off her arguments like flies. I'm
straining to understand, but the señora seems convinced about
the treasure, and maybe with good reason. San Miguel de Allende
was founded in 1542 as a way station on the dangerous Antiguo
Camino Real, the route the mule trains took from the gold and
mainly silver mines of Guanajuato and Zacatecas to Mexico City.
There were no banks in those days, so over the years, as the little
town grew, the workers and bandits did what people have done
with treasure forever: they buried it in their backyards. The turquoise house and its backyard have existed for more than two
hundred years; prior to that, it was probably part of a larger property before it was divided up into workers' row houses. It's entirely possible someone buried a stash there.

Finally the elderly woman's son seems to have convinced
her to sell. She's sitting back in the chair, resigned, her feet not
touching the floor, her shawl pulled tightly around her crossed
arms. The son may have argued that it would, after all, take a
great deal of buried silver to make up for the amount of money
I am prepared to pay, in cash, for the house. They're asking the
equivalent of 350 pounds of silver for the lot, which is more than
you'd get if you turned the entire artisans' market upside down
and shook.

Before the señora can change her mind, I try to distract her
by making polite conversation in Spanish, asking how many chil-

dren and grandchildren she has—so many, she's not sure—and
when she lived in the house. She doesn't seem to be nostalgic for
the place; eleven people were crammed inside those walls. But she
smiles and I smile back, and when everybody's smiling the attorney gets up to get the papers to sign. The deal's going to go
through.

The attorney is gone for an inordinately long time, but this is
Mexico, and while everyone else goes back to whispering in Spanish—the law office has the silent solemnity of a church—I sit
there, considering that when I sign the papers, I'll be committed.
It's a great deal of money to pay for a tiny bit of land in Mexico,
especially since it's everything I have, all that I've managed to accumulate writing hundreds of magazine articles at a dollar or two
a word. I'm picturing fifty thousand words stacked up like bricks
in that little lot. I will have nothing left in stocks or money market
funds, no diversification, and PBS financial gurus will be scolding
me in my dreams. I'll no longer be able to buy expensive shoes
or airplane tickets to Italy or get my hair highlighted—except,
maybe, in Mexico. I'm putting all my *huevos* in one *cesto*.

Finally the portly attorney returns, with no papers, and says
something I don't understand. The elderly woman raises her
hands to the skies, and her son rolls his eyes. They both shake
their heads in disgust.

It turns out the attorney has done what I'm paying him for;
he's uncovered a lien against the building that, had the sale gone
through, I would have been responsible for paying. Some nephew,
a good-for-nothing *borracho* from what I can tell from his relatives' expressions, took out a loan on the house, which wasn't his

to begin with, but the money is owed, and must be paid, before the house is sold.

Abruptly, everyone gets up from the chairs, we shake hands all around, and the meeting is over. Outside, I ask Roberto what's going to happen next, whether I'll get the house. *¿Quién sabe?* "This sort of thing happens all the time," he says. It could be the reason the house has been abandoned for so long, why the FOR SALE sign looks like an antique.

I'M DISAPPOINTED I can't buy the house. Maybe I've dodged a big mess. And maybe the idea of buying the house, and the excitement I felt about it, alerted me to a new possibility in my life, beyond the Hippie Apartment in the Haight, which I should explore. The turquoise house can't be the last one for sale in the centro, but I'm not going to look any farther for now. I'm going home the day after tomorrow.

To distract myself, I go back to being a tourist and visit the Sanctuary of Atotonilco, just fifteen minutes outside San Miguel. I tag along with a group and wander around the church, which, with its all-over frescoes, has been called the Sistine Chapel of the Americas. The artist didn't have Michelangelo's cheerful disposition, though; there's no benevolent God surrounded by happy cherubs giving Adam a loving look as he's about to touch his finger and awaken him to the glory of the world. Atotonilco is covered with fierce demons, dark angels, and suffering saints, with a gruesome bleeding Christ as the centerpiece. Some 100,000 pilgrims make it to this Mexican Baroque masterpiece per year, most of them on their scraped and bloodied knees or flagellating themselves. The place has woeful vibes, making me think perhaps I don't want to be in this part of the world anyway. I'd rather be back in Italy, where the cherubs are fat, the angels are well tended, and the art makes you think that the world, for whatever miseries its lovely saints have suffered, is essentially a beautiful, not evil, place.

As the tour guide lectures the group under the church's salmon-colored arches, I wander back to the van and chat with Martín, the driver, a short, upbeat man who is about my age. His English is excellent, but I try to speak Spanish anyway because we're in Mexico.

I ask him where in town he grew up. "Calle Loreto," he says. His mother still lives on the street and makes the best tortillas in town.

"I think that's my favorite street in San Miguel," I tell him. I have pretty much let go of my fantasy about the turquoise house on that street, but not quite.

Martín left San Miguel to work and settled back here after several forays to the United States, to Kentucky, where he worked construction and many other jobs. I presume he crossed into the country illegally—so many of the people in this town risk their lives to go make a few more dollars per hour in the United States—and ask him if it was difficult.

Sí, sí, he says, *muy difícil,* and I can tell that's an understatement. He crossed the border several times, and a few of them were very dangerous. He's been lost, parched, shot at, hidden from border patrols, and had to catch food to survive, eating armadillos and snakes, and glad to have them.

"Were there lots of rattlesnakes?" I ask, shuddering.

"Everywhere."

Martín is offhand in his manner, but there is something so dark in his answers that I ask if anyone ever died crossing the border with him. I'm not prepared for his answer. Once, he set off with thirteen other people, including a *coyote* they each paid $1,500 to lead them, draining the family coffers, borrowing from everyone, incurring high-interest loans. None of them brought along much water or food because they were told to travel light, it was going to take just a couple hours to reach their destination. Some of them carried just a bottle of Coke. Martín, who had crossed the border before—the first time was when he was fourteen years old—took a full knapsack and lagged behind the group. At some point they stopped for a siesta, and when Martín awoke he discovered that the rest of the group had left him, abandoned in the middle of nowhere. He called out and walked in every direction, but he was absolutely alone. With no *coyote* to guide him, he was lost in the middle of the vast Sonoran Desert, where every saguaro cactus looked the same and there were no landmarks and no shade or shelter from the relentless sun. He wandered for several days, surviving with what food and water he had brought, resting during the day and setting out after dusk, trying to avoid nocturnal scorpions and sidewinders. By the end he was burned, beyond thirst, staggering, and seeing visions. His feet were bleeding, his arms and legs infected by cactus spines. A border patrol—the enemy, the savior—picked him up just in time, offered him water and food, and sent him back across the border. The other thirteen people in his group, he eventually learned, had all died of heat exposure, every one.

"*Lo siento mucho.*" There's nothing to say but I'm sorry. I look back at Atotonilco, whose bloody, violent murals reflect the harsh history of this place. It's a brutal, unfair land. It is so easy for me to get on a plane and come to Mexico, so dangerous for people who cross over to build our houses and pick our vegetables and grapes, keeping our prices low. And the gringos in San Miguel de Allende, it must be said, are profiting from the huge disparity in wealth between the countries, living easy here on a lot less. It's complicated, of course: they're bringing jobs and raising wages, too, so fewer people have to cross the border. Martín is able to stay in the town he grew up in and loves instead of crossing the border, he says, because he makes a good living driving a tour van. Good and bad.

The group at Atotonilco has finished with the lecture and is now shopping at the souvenir stands nearby. "I guess God wanted you to survive," I say to Martín. "He had plans for you."

He smiles. "*Gracias a Dios,*" he says.

AFTER THE TOUR, Martín drops the group off near the jardín, and the rest of the people scatter. I sit down at an outside table of a café on the corner and order my favorite dish, tortilla soup, with smoky chipotle peppers, strips of avocado, and tortilla shreds, along with a beer. I watch the people in the jardín, which is constantly active, and look up at the Gothic-style La Parroquia, almost comic in its faux-European splendor. I wonder, after I leave in a couple of days, whether I'll ever come back here. It's been wonderful to revisit a place from my childhood, to feel its emotional tug, and exciting to think about buying something here, to consider settling in a foreign but friendly place. But I'll be traveling on.

I drain my beer and my cell phone rings, which startles me, since hardly anyone has called me on it. I bought it right after I made an offer on the house, thinking I'd need it, and now it'll go into the drawer at home with a bunch of other cheap international cell phones and chips.

"*Bueno?*" I answer.

It's Roberto. He tells me the family has paid the lien on the building and I can come sign the papers. The turquoise house is mine.

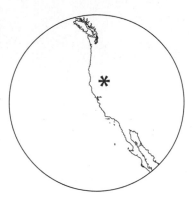

Chapter Fifteen

SAN FRANCISCO *
SAN MIGUEL DE ALLENDE

2007-2008

At home in San Francisco, I'm stirring a big pot of tortilla soup, setting out plates of tamales, slicing up avocados, squeezing limes for margaritas, waiting for guests to arrive at my birthday dinner.

This year, Guillermo isn't here. I feel his absence keenly, not only because his Peruvian tamales are so much better than the Mexican ones I bought but because he is unable to travel, still not quite himself after a drunk driver mowed him down while he was out running a few months ago. Things happen that fast. But despite the fact that initially the neurologist in the ICU lamented how bad his MRI looked and whispered that he might not speak or walk again, he is more or less out of the fog, missing a margin of intelligence that only he is smart enough to know has disappeared, a softening of the edges that actually makes him easier to be around. (It also somehow helps him fall in love, get married, and have a baby boy, named after the father he lost in the jungle, only a year later.)

The doorbell rings, friends arrive, and I start pouring margaritas. Chatting in the kitchen, I tell them the news, that I've bought a little property in San Miguel. Then I tell them *how* little.

Marc shakes his head. "You can build San Miguel's first bowling alley." He grins. "But they'll have to take turns for the lane."

"Baguettes," Axil chimes in. "It's perfect for baking baguettes."

"It's going to be great," says Sandra, putting an arm around my shoulder. She looks at the guys. "I mean, it's almost as wide as this kitchen."

I take a few sips of my margarita and ask Peppe, a construction engineer, if he thinks it's possible to build a house on a lot that narrow. He laughs, asks if I considered that before I bought it, and then, seeing my anxious face, swipes his hand over his smooth head and reconsiders. "*È possibile,*" he says. "*Ma sarà un bel problema.*" Possible, but it'll be a nice problem.

Possible is good enough. I'm not going to worry about the house. It's a party, I'm surrounded by my friends, and I'm much cheerier at forty-six than I was on my forty-fifth birthday.

I'VE SENT A check for the house to Mexico, and after waiting several weeks—repeatedly e-mailing Roberto, who writes, "Relax and go eat a gordita"—I finally get a receipt, a deed, and a key to the house. I have no clue what to do next. I recall Sue, a new friend in San Miguel who married her nineteen-year-old Mexican student when she was teaching English there in her early thirties, telling me that the tradition is to have campfire parties on a property where you can't afford to build. The lot may just sit empty for a few more years, as it has for the past thirty; I'll bring down marshmallows.

Financing construction of a house in Mexico when you don't

own anything in the United States turns out to be tricky. Some people, I realize, would have discovered that before they bought the property. When I walk into my bank on Haight Street and sit down to talk to the ponytailed loan officer, he points out that I have no collateral and nothing with which to secure a loan, because property in Mexico isn't something the bank can easily seize.

"Dude," he says, spreading his palms on the desk. "There's, like, no way."

I make some calls and find companies that do construction loans in Mexico, but their fees and rates are exorbitant, and most insist that you use their contractors, who, judging from the Web sites, build only peach-toned faux-Mediterranean villas with Ionic columns, decorated with giant inlaid seashells. My best option seems to be to open a bunch of credit cards, pay for the construction with cash advances, then declare bankruptcy and run off to, um, Mexico.

I finally turn to the Bank of Mom and Dad. I've never asked my parents for a loan, partly because, growing up poor in the Depression era, both with single mothers who were teachers, they have a bootstrap mentality about money. But I come up with a plan to pay them the interest they're making on their other investments, ask a lawyer how to make it all official, and present it to them, explaining how my experience in San Miguel de Allende as a child helped shape who I am, and how I am, in some ways, coming full circle.

To my surprise, they agree to the deal and seem happy about the prospect of my finally having a place of my own. They're worried about the details of how it will all work out and ask a lot of questions, but I also get the sense that they're glad, since they're a little bored in their retirement after extremely busy careers, to have a stake in an interesting project. It makes me feel content to know that though I don't have a partner to rely on in my life, I have my family. (A year later, when stocks crash, my parents are pleased that they took the money out of the market and are getting reliable interest on a loan.)

Designing the house is much more fun to think about but also a challenge, since I've never done anything more imaginative, spacewise, than paint a room yellow or move the piano to the other wall. It stretches unused muscles to visualize building a small house, calling forth spatial relations skills I haven't used since I packed a carry-on suitcase to spend three weeks during winter in Egypt, London, and Ireland. I buy books on small spaces, sketch a lot of long, wobbly rectangles in my notebook, play with putting the kitchen here or there, and wonder where there will be room for stairs.

However small the house, the project seems huge to do alone. With no experience in the realm of architecture or design, the only thing I have in my corner is a sure sense of taste. Good or bad, whatever anyone else thinks, at forty-six you have developed your style. Architecture and decor have to be a lot like fashion or art: at a certain point you're confident about what you like and what suits you, and you're less apt to make mistakes you regret. So I decide to just trust what I like.

I head back to San Miguel in March and start looking around at other houses as models. Unfortunately, the house I like the most, owned by my friend Jody—built around ruins in the centro, modern but using historic materials—is huge and worth millions. It ruins me for other houses. It's like a painting—you can't help it, you fall in love. I want a miniature by that same artist. Jody tells me the architect is named Anja, and asking around, I learn that her reputation is that she's good but expensive.

I try other architects and designers who might be cheaper. In each house, I sense that something's wrong, unharmonious, too phony colonial. When a young Mexican architect who does modern, minimal houses comes to visit the house and I open the door, I've forgotten how really small it is.

"Well, you can do *something* here," he says gloomily. "Maybe a spiral staircase." He isn't enthusiastic and doesn't come up with any sketches or plans, as promised, to bid on the job. When we leave the house, I feel uneasy; maybe I've made a disastrous decision.

I finally call Anja, introduce myself, and tell her I've bought a little house on Calle Loreto.

"The turquoise one?" she asks and says she's inquired about the house herself (I meet many others in town who tried to buy the house, one woman for five years, with no one answering the calls; I got lucky, or, as they say in San Miguel, it was Meant to Be). "Great location," Anja says, and we make an appointment to meet.

Given her talent and reputation, I expect someone older than the lively Mexican woman in her early thirties who walks into the café. She kisses the owner, then greets me and sits down with me. She's warm but all business, describing her process, which involves taking measurements, drawing plans, obtaining permits, and overseeing the construction. She makes quick sketches in her notebook with perfectly straight rectangles. She seems to be competent at everything I'm not.

Anja asks how big the lot is, *más o menos*. This is where I've lost the other architects' interest, when they've told me there's no way to build more than one bedroom, where the subtext is that it just isn't worth their time.

"Three and a half by fourteen meters," I say. I drain my coffee, ready to get up and leave.

Anja lights up, clasping her hands together. "We can make a little, what do you call that, where you put your *joyería*?"

"A jewel box?"

"*Sí, sí!* We're going to build a little jewel box!"

AND SO WE DO.

Most stories—maybe every story—about building a house in a foreign country are full of drama, disasters, crumbling ceilings, pipes bursting, thieving neighbors, insect infestations, and contractors running off with cash, leaving things half finished. But from the beginning, Anja and I have a seamless and delightful collaboration, our flurries of ideas easily settling down and taking shape.

She starts by drawing up a wish list of all the things I want in my house. This is much more satisfying than making a list of all the qualities you want in your dream man, sending your intention out into the universe so that he will magically show up. This is concrete. So I begin with the general—a great kitchen and writing studio, some outdoor spaces to sit in the sun, two bedrooms—and move on to specifics such as a knife drawer in the kitchen island, wine shelves tucked into the dining room bench, reading lights over the bed, and a napping couch in my office.

A few weeks later, Anja sends watercolor plans to San Francisco that astound me—she has managed to put everything into my little house, while making it feel spare. I show them to my friend Peppe for an expert opinion; after looking at Anja's drawings, he tells me I'm in good hands, asks if she's cute and single, then begins referring to her as "*La mia fidanzata messicana,*" my Mexican girlfriend.

But when I return to San Miguel in a few months to check in on the house during the "*obras negras,*" the black works, the initial brick and concrete construction, the tiny place is heaped with bags of material and litter. What have I done? The place where the kitchen is supposed to go is a dark, dank hole. Nothing of the original house, two hundred years old, is usable, except the front mesquite door and the interior doors, even the bricks are rotted through. I'm claustrophobic in the space.

"*No te preocupe,*" says Anja, laughing, don't worry. Then she takes me up the zigzagging stairs, with no railing yet, to the top terrace. I have no idea what the view from up there will be. It turns out to be sweeping, with all of San Miguel at our feet. "Look," Anja says, pointing. "You can see the Parroquia from here."

We scramble back down to the bottom of the construction site, which I eye nervously. "Let's go pick out tiles," Anja says, dismissing the mess.

*   *   *

FROM THE START of construction, Finn insists I stay at her
house whenever I'm in town. Hers is a rambling colonial place,
with odd twists and turns, built as a party house for the property
next door, later inhabited by elderly ladies who insisted that fairies live there; Finn's three-year-old daughter, Tallulah, is careful not to pick the leaves off the plants because that's where the
ladies said the fairies hide. There is always a little bit of magic
in the air: Tallulah and her friends Alejandra and Fernanda
put on princess dresses and run around casting spells in Spanish, Finn takes her energy healer as seriously as her accountant
and personal trainer, birds twitter, I play Mary Poppins songs on
the grand piano for the children, and some days I think Bogart
the Bijon Frise will start speaking French and Phoebe the mutt
will answer back in street Spanish. Every morning I get kisses
from the girls, the first of many kisses I'll get from friends in
Mexico all day long. The atmosphere feels light, feminine, twin-
kly, and happy.

   Finn uses my visit as an excuse to throw a party, with a *Breakfast at Tiffany's* theme, and the place is packed with men in skinny
ties and women in little black dresses wearing giant cocktail
rings, gringos and Mexicans alike, all waving long cigarette hold-
ers and dancing to a swanky jazz band until the early morning.
Under their costumes they reveal themselves to be artists, designers, massage therapists, pastry chefs, party planners, teachers. One
woman comes as Frida Kahlo, complete with a monobrow, which
confuses me, themewise, until someone explains that she dresses

like that all the time. There are clearly a lot of fun-loving people
in this town, as well as more than a few eccentrics.

As my house takes shape, so does the community around
me. At times, I worry that as enchanted as I am with the town,
I might not fit in with its people. Friends in San Francisco have
questioned why someone who travels to remote parts of the world
would buy a house in such a gringo-infested town. Indeed, I run
across retirees who've built dream houses that, aside from the cost,
might as well be in suburban Texas; some scarcely bother to learn
enough Spanish to say "*Gracias.*" I see women in heavy jewelry
whose puppet faces display their penchant for cheap plastic surgery. There are "healers" who seem to have attained their degrees
by dint of crossing the border, throwing on a shawl, and listening
to a few Eckhart Tolle tapes. But there are people in every town
who are not your crowd, and there are few enough of them in San
Miguel that they're easy to avoid.

There are also people like me here, who want to mingle in
another culture, learn to speak another language, soak up the colors and sun, and work on creative projects and who recognize
that it isn't easy for a single woman in her forties to plop herself
down in any town in Italy or Mexico, that she would be too much
of an outsider, and too alone, without a community of others who
have ventured here before her. There's a balance between what's
foreign and familiar, what's daring and safe.

The more time I spend in San Miguel, the more depth I find
in the people I encounter. The cafés are full of artists and photographers, and many of them are serious about their work, some
world class. Just as the plain faces of the houses in San Miguel

hide magnificent courtyards and whimsical houses, you never know what kinds of talents you'll find in the people you pass on the streets. The town is a playground for architects, whose clients let them run wild with their creative visions. The theme of self-invention that I first came here to explore for my article is repeated everywhere, as I meet more and more people—women, in particular—who have moved here after one phase of their lives has ended, whether because they have divorced, their children have grown, their jobs are over, or they simply want a change, to take a leap into something new, something truer to who they want to be in the latter part of their lives; most are much happier as a result. Many expatriates create programs for the community—midwifery schools, collective child care centers for young Mexican working women, kitchens in the camp to feed schoolchildren, dance classes to build young girls' confidence, rescue groups for the town's innumerable little stray mutts. One friend who started a writers' conference here asks me to teach. Others immerse themselves in Mexican folk art, history, or indigenous communities. The town isn't divided into gringos and Mexicans, as I originally feared, or young and old; I find myself collecting an international group of friends of all ages.

I feel certain I'm in the right community when one evening, out walking with Finn, I notice a sign up for African dance. I take a class with the Senegalese teacher, Lamine, a giraffe of a man with dreadlocks, and am amazed to find a world-class dancer in San Miguel who has taught with some of the best companies in New York. At the end of the class, he tells me, in his simple African way, touching his heart, flashing a brilliant smile, that I am a good person. "African dance is your medicine," he says, and he's right; I dance to a joyful, exhausted sweat every time I'm in town, as I haven't danced since those afternoons in college, and think of my luck to have found it here. Lamine and I become friends, and I like to cook for him, since he misses chicken and rice dishes from Senegal and it makes him, too, feel as if he's at home to share a meal.

Besides African dance, there are salsa lessons; the men encourage me, lead me softly, and smile at my mistakes in dance steps or the language. (One day, a local shopkeeper asks me out, and when I hesitate and tell him I need to learn salsa—*aprender la salsa*—he offers to come over to my house with a tomato, onion, and peppers). My Spanish—and my salsa dancing (*aprender* bailar *la salsa*)—get better, *poco a poco,* until one evening with Mexican friends, singing karaoke and dancing until three in the morning, I realize I haven't spoken English all night, except the words to the Patsy Cline songs. When one of the men, Ricardo, asks me to dance, for the first time I stop worrying and let him lead, and we spin around, perfectly in time. People clap when we're done. "Not bad," Ricardo says, "for a gringa."

As my house is being built, I realize San Miguel is a wonderful jumping-off point for all of Latin America. I sign up for Lamine's African dance workshop in Tulum, dancing each day in a huge palapa by the beach, and realize how close the ocean is to San Miguel. I tag along with Deb, a folk art specialist who owns a local store with her husband, Rick, to Pátzcuaro, where they take me with them to artisan villages that circle the lake, each making its own distinctive pottery, masks, or copperware, each with its own culture and history. I've barely dipped into Mexico City or tasted its increasingly renowned cuisine; there's so much of Mexico I don't know and am so eager to explore.

THE HOUSE TAKES about a year to build, slightly longer and more expensive than expected, but Mexico is a good place to practice patience. Whenever someone is an hour or a day late, I try to think of it as an opportunity to step out of my constant sense of urgency, to relax. There is, in fact, a mindfulness to day-to-day encounters in Mexico, an attentive cordiality, that is contagious. You see it in the politeness people pay to one another, automatically. Drivers wait good-naturedly for pedestrians and other cars at intersections. People take the time to stop in the street and greet one another, with no sense of hurry. There is endless Mexican patience for things that can always be a little late, go a little wrong, but will work themselves out tomorrow.

WHEN I RETURN to San Miguel for the third visit in a year and the house is almost done, Anja has sent me photos of the construction and every receipt for every brick, so I know what to expect. But when she opens the mesquite doors, and I walk into a shimmering entryway, with tall glass-and-wrought-iron doors that open to an atrium to the sky, sculptural white stairs, terracotta tiles, a gourmet kitchen with lit polished concrete shelves and a big prep island, a thirteen-foot wood desk in my studio with a napping couch, three terraces, with beautiful details, I'm amazed. We've turned the smallest lot in San Miguel into a jewel box. Everyone—architects, the guy who delivers water, the up-holsterer, the rug maker, the gas man, the Internet installer, the neighbors, my friends—is astonished when they open those two-hundred-year-old wooden doors.

Anja and I go to an Italian restaurant in an old hacienda in the country to celebrate finishing the house. We start with a glass of champagne. *"Felicitaciones,"* I say, *"y gracias."* Anja has been very patient with my speaking Spanish as long as it holds out, especially since her English is nearly perfect.

"Congratulations," she says. "This has been wonderful, so easy." We both dab our eyes with our napkins and laugh at each other for crying. I may be the only person who's ever built a house in Mexico who wishes the construction would never end.

When I move my suitcases out of Finn's house, I tell Tallu-lah, now four, that she can come visit me at my new house. With a grave expression, she puts her hands on her waist, above her pink tutu. "Mom," she asks Finn, "why does Laura have to go live somewhere else when she can live right here with us?"

AS SOON AS I move into my house, I have a sense that it fits me just right, like a custom suit. It's small but seems airy and spa-cious. I feel settled and calm, productive in my quiet office. I try to keep the house spare and furnish it, as much as possible—rugs, stools, glassware, ceramics—from the nearby mercado and the merchants on my street. My main worry is that I will run out of English books, but that would probably be just as well, since I should start reading Spanish.

Over the next two months, I grow accustomed to the roosters

that wake me every morning and sleep through the fireworks and ranchero music that can last all night. I learn the names of the people who live on my street and tell them *"Buenos días"* every morning; I say *"Buenas noches"* to the teenage couple who makes out in my doorway every night. There are rhythms to the week: Luis, the farmer, brings me organic vegetables on Fridays, and I make them into soup on Saturday. I go swimming in the nearby hot springs or to yoga in the mornings, or hike up the canyon to the botanical gardens. In the afternoon, I love to watch the tropical rain pour into the atrium of my house and dash through the downpour to make a cup of tea in the kitchen. I work quietly during the days and then find someone to eat *comida* with in the evenings or some place to listen to live music or dance. When the Day of the Dead comes, with bright marigolds attracting the dead to altars with their favorite foods, photos, and beloved possessions, I walk to the cemetery with people laughing, crying, and playing music and think I must start collecting objects—a photo of Maya, my grandmother's rhinestone earrings—that remind me of my own departed friends and family, so that I, too, can visit with them once a year.

It sometimes seems to me that there was a little magic involved in ending up in this little house in Mexico. The sense of magic and coincidence that pervades San Miguel de Allende, exaggerated by New Age types, can nevertheless be hard to explain. The town feels a little sparkly around the edges, and people are in the habit of speaking about unseen energies, which I am not. Yet whether it is magic or middle age, I am realizing that intention has a lot to do with how things turn out, and accomplish-

ments don't always have to involve such a difficult personal fight
or even campaign. So, too, how you tell your story has a great deal
to do with how you feel about the circumstances in your life and
which direction your story is going to go in. In a peaceful, patient
town, surrounded by friends, I am losing the threads of my story
that have to do with disappointment, with regret, with difficulties
with men. I am happy for the wonderful men I have in my life,
would be happy for a new love, and am happy either way. That is
a kind of magical thinking that works.

The more people I meet here, the more I see them finding
the magic in their own lives. One woman tells me that despite
the skewed ratio of women to men here—some say it's thirteen
to one—all the formerly single women she knows have met their
husbands while they were passing through town. Others couldn't
care less about relationships and find other kinds of satisfying
companionship or spiritual practices or bursts of creative talent.
There is something here that allows people to rewrite their lives,
take risks, and tap their long-simmering talents. There is something about having built a little house that makes me feel settled
and grounded, not always tempted to fly away but ready to explore something new, discover something deeper.

Sometimes the magic in San Miguel startles me. One evening
I am having a glass of wine, waiting for a friend at a bar, and
chat with a couple next to me, who just met in Spanish class. I
ask them about themselves; she is traveling for a few months and
happened to end up here, and he is reluctant to say what he does.
That makes me curious, so I press, and he quietly admits that he
is a shaman—it isn't his fault, he used to be a high school math

teacher, but it just turns out that it's a talent he has, he can see things and sometimes fix them.

"What kinds of things?" I ask. I am skeptical, to say the least, but his reluctance to talk makes him seem honest.

"Physical things, emotional things," he says. "I just see them."

I can't resist asking him what he sees about me. We are in a dim outdoor space, and the bar is between us; he can't see more than my upper body.

"Your right hip," he says, immediately. "It was injured a few years ago, and it's still injured. You've tried everything, but the pain deep down doesn't go away. You have trouble sitting cross-legged."

I'm speechless. He hasn't seen me walk, and even if he had, no one can detect my injury.

"How did it happen?" I ask, pushing my luck.

He frowns. "I don't think you want me to talk about that right now," he says. "It's a very personal story."

"Right," I say.

"What is it?" asks the young woman with him.

"Nothing," the shaman and I say in unison.

"Can you fix it?" I ask.

"I already did," he says.

I rotate my hip joint and still feel the pain.

"I know," he says. "It'll take a few days. You'll wake up Tuesday morning, and it'll be fine."

Tuesday morning, despite believing that I will be better, my hip still hurts. Maybe a little less. On Thursday, I have a party in my new house, everyone squeezed together in the little kitchen or hanging out on the terrace for a smoke, and I see the shaman and give him a kiss on the cheek.

"I know," he says, before I say anything. "It's still there."

I nod.

"I was a little drunk, and you were behind the bar," he says, sheepishly.

"No worries," I say. He's like a good-natured warlock who gets things a little wrong, like the befuddled aunt on *Bewitched* accidentally turning Darrin into a toad.

"I can try again," he says, not moving. "I just did."

"Sometimes pain is there for a reason," I say. "It can serve as a reminder." I have a deep, physical twinge that tells me I'm vulnerable, that it's okay to be vulnerable, to want to protect myself and to be protected. It reminds me I'm female, that I've lived a full and exciting life, that I've made mistakes, that I've forgiven myself and others, that I do my best, here in middle age, to live with Mexican patience, tango receptivity, and a Spirit Rock sense of lovingkindness.

"That's true," says the shaman.

"I mean, if you *can* make it disappear, go for it."

AFTER EACH VISIT to San Miguel, when I come home to San Francisco, my friends tell me I look good and seem softer and more relaxed, as if I've just been on a meditation retreat. After spending some weeks in Mexico, I always fall in love with San Francisco anew—for its wonderful restaurants, huge parks, steep hills, longtime friends, and intellectual liveliness (people are much less apt to use the phrase "It's all up to the universe" in conversation, for instance). I'm not ready to give up San Francisco. When I'm back in the Bay Area I realize that it's my home; San Miguel is a getaway, *tranquilo,* a place where I love to spend some of my time, to speak a little Spanish and feel a little Mexican, but it doesn't have San Francisco's stimulation. Yet when I'm in San Miguel, it feels like home, too, I feel softer and more at ease when I'm there, and I wonder how I can leave. I am grateful to have both, to feel settled but able to see my surroundings, in either place, with the fresh eyes of a traveler.

I SEND PHOTOS of my house to the Professor and tell him I hope he comes visit sometime. He e-mails me back saying congratulations, it's beautiful, and who knows when he may find himself in Mexico. He sends wishes that Obama will win the presidency, saying it would be magnificent, once again the entire world could be friends with the United States. I'm happy to hear from him; he has not written since last summer, when he told me he was going on a trip to India, which he had always wanted to visit, telling me that if his money didn't hold out in Paris, he'd retire there in style.

And then he tells me he has bad news.

He has been diagnosed with cancer, and the doctors have given him two rounds of chemotherapy. He won't be able to go back to the university, not this year. "I had hoped," he writes, "to at least reach sixty-five before finding myself in this situation."

He is now fifty-nine, and I am almost the age he was when

we first met, when he was such a sexy, assured older man. But still so young.

I call him in Paris, and when a woman answers I try to come up with the polite way in French to say good afternoon and ask to speak to the Professor. He comes to the phone and first I forget and say hello in Spanish and then Italian and he realizes it's me. "*Laura,*" he says, the rolling Italian way, the way he first pronounced it after we met, over breakfast at a pensione on Ischia, on our way together already to go see the view of the sea from the highest point on the island. "It's so nice to hear your voice," he says, always so sweet, sounding so close.

I stumble over my words, I'm so sorry, and I can't say anything for what seems a long time, from Mexico to France, but I want to pull myself together because I don't want him to think that I'm so upset, as if that would makes things worse.

"*È così,*" he says. It's like that.

I try to cheerfully tell him a little bit about Mexico and the election, how wonderful that everyone is so excited. We talk about his son, who is thinking about coming to San Francisco, and he asks if I will help him, and I say of course, anything, but a nineteen-year-old who is nearly as handsome and charming as his father won't need any help at all. He laughs.

I ask about his trip to India. It was beautiful, incredible, he says, from north to south, and a good thing that he traveled when he did. If he had known, he never would have gone, never would have experienced the place he dreamed about for so long. When he returned home, he had a pain in his stomach. I don't want to ask, but he offers that it is liver cancer, not an easy kind, but he is feeling okay for now. He has many friends who visit and care for him and keep him company, and he is full of hope. I ask if he is still with the same woman, and he says, "The same beautiful woman, *meno male,*" a good thing, so I know she is nearby, listening, and I'm so glad she is there for him.

He asks if I have any romances, and I say nothing right now. *Niente.*

"I can't believe that," he says.

"We'll see," I say. "Someone always turns up."

I tell him I send him a big, big hug and kiss and say I hope that all this will be nothing, a small, forgettable episode in *la bella vita.* As I say it, I believe it to be true.

"*Grazie, bella,*" he says. He asks if maybe I have plans to come to Europe sometime soon. I say I don't know, but of course I always love to come to Europe, and we say "*Ciao, ciao, ciao,*" many times, the way the Italians say good-bye, reluctant to hang up.

I climb the stairs to the terrace, hear the ranchero music playing from next door, then a child's laugh and a rooster's crow, and sit with the warm rays of sunshine drying my face. I spend a long time like that, trying to breathe evenly. Church bells ring, and dogs bark in response.

In a little while, I will go see about booking a ticket to Paris, to visit an old friend, a love, a piece of my heart. But for now I am just going to sit in the sun.

By late fall, the plants in my house have grown, delicate periwinkle vines dripping down the atrium, lavender and jasmine blooming, cactus and aloe plants growing into Dr. Seussian proportions. My parents have decided to visit for my mom's eightieth birthday.

This wasn't an easy decision; since she's been diagnosed with Parkinson's, it's been more difficult for my mother to travel comfortably. It dismays her not to have new adventures to recount to her friends; it makes her feel less like herself, though her friends know she has a lifetime of being quietly daring. I tell Mom and Dad it's easier to get to Mexico than it was when we came in 1971; instead of taking a crowded bus from Mexico City, a driver meets you at the León airport with a sign with your name on it and drives you directly to my house.

When they arrive, they open the door and are astonished at the enchantment that makes eleven feet wide seem so huge. Though they've been following the progress in photos, they say they could never imagine how much better it is in person, and right away they're glad they came. My father, a perfectionist, admires the craftsmanship, the wrought iron and the wood cabinets, and pronounces himself impressed. After they explore the house, Mom calls my sister and has tears in her eyes. "It's just wonderful," she says. "Darn it, maybe it's the Parkinson's, it makes me cry."

In the morning we wander around town, Mom with her walking stick to maneuver the cobblestones. I explain that on the narrow sidewalks, as an elderly woman, she is at the top of the sidewalk hierarchy and never has to give way to someone else (men step off the sidewalk for women, younger women make way for older women or those burdened with bags or children). Mom and Dad don't recognize anything about the town until we come to the blue-doored bakery, and then La Parroquia, and then everything suddenly seems familiar.

Over the next few days I show them this world they introduced me to so many years ago. We have breakfast with Finn and lunch with Anja, we visit Jody's house, as well as folk art galleries, an artist's mosaic-covered house, and photography collections. Dad practices his Spanish running errands to the hardware store, to buy groceries, to get a paper. On Mom's birthday, we take a taxi up to the Charco, the botanical gardens, and she is in her favorite kind of place, a cool and sunny blooming desert. We have lunch in La Aurora design center with Finn, drinking wine at noon, and Mom agrees, at this time of life when she is trying to throw everything away, to let Dad buy her a necklace.

In the evening, we go to a party in a Frida Kahlo–colored house, where a friendly group gathers on the roof, and Mom and Dad mingle with these latter-day hippies and artists. When it gets cold, we all go inside, and the hostess gets up to make a speech, greeting everyone, celebrating birthdays and weddings and visits, saying she's grateful for her friends and the wonderful place we all live in. "Paradise," she says.

Then she asks if anyone has anything else to say, and I offer that it's my mom's eightieth birthday, and that I want to thank her for having had the daring and foresight to bring me and my sisters here thirty-five years ago, when it was difficult to do so. "That trip," I tell the group, "had a lot to do with making me who I am, with me being back in San Miguel today." They all clap for Mom, who deserves a toast and a party, even among friendly strangers, on her eightieth birthday.

On our way home, Mom is tired, and she leans on my father, who, hearty and handsome, still seems fifteen years younger than his age. All my friends have remarked on how charming my father is, and though I appreciate how personable he's become in his later years, my mother isn't able, any more, to fully project who she is to new people, her vitality and passions. I wonder if I'll have someone to lean on when I'm older, someone who will take my arm and cherish the fullness of me—the curious wanderer and the woman who likes to stay home, chop vegetables, and hear compliments about her cooking—even when I'm no longer able to dance, to flirt, to pack my bags at the last minute and board a plane.

"I love you," my parents each say to me, as we hug and they step into the taxi at the end of the night. It's a phrase I hear and say more often the older I get, and I take that as a good sign.

In fall 2009, I was in Europe for a couple of months and wrote to the Professor to say I'd like to visit him in Paris. He replied that he was in the hospital—"the least sexy place in the world"—and suggested I come later, when he was recovered from surgery. After a few weeks, he was still in the hospital, and this time he said sure, why don't you come by, and gave me the room number.

When I knocked, the nurse opened the door and asked me to wait a few minutes. In that brief flash, I'd glimpsed what the Professor looked like now, and I was glad for the chance to collect myself. When I returned, he was on his feet, IV trailing, hugging me and telling me what a pleasure it was to see me. His curly locks were shorn and dark from indoor light; he was all ribs and sunken cheeks, but he was there.

We chatted for a couple of hours, and I returned a second day. He told me I looked the same, and I said he was handsome with a beard, small stretches to remind us of our younger, sexier selves. I talked about the Poussin paintings I'd recently seen at the Hermitage—a favorite among the many artists he acquainted me with—and reminisced about our travels, but he waved away the topic. "I think that part of my life is over," he said. So we spoke of ordinary things. He showed me photos of his wedding and children, and I showed him pictures of Golden Gate Park on a spring morning. I described an amusing art exhibit I'd seen that morning at the Pompidou and thanked him for teaching me so much about how to experience art.

I was cheerful, maybe too cheerful. But the Professor laughed at my stories and then caught himself laughing. "This is the first time I've forgotten I'm sick," he said, marveling. "You make me feel good, like myself."

He thanked me for making a special trip.

"Any trip to Paris is special," I said.

He held my hand. "Some relationships, *cara,* are important for life."

He asked if I was seeing anyone, if I was in love, and I told him I have bad luck with men. Seeing him, hearing his still-vibrant voice, I wondered if I was still single, after all these years, because he always had been in my life, and in my heart. At least I'd never met another man I loved as much.

The Professor said he was looking forward to going home soon. The cancer was inoperable, but these days they treat it like a chronic disease.

"Like AIDS," I said, wanting to believe it.

"*Brava,*" he said.

I kissed him on each cheek and reminded him that he always said we never knew when or where we were going to see each other again.

"*Spero che ci vediamo,*" he said. I hope we'll see each other again.

"*Ci vediamo,*" I said, glad there's no other way to say good-bye in Italian. I walked out of the hospital, and kept on walking, all the way across gray Paris, from Montparnasse to Montmartre.

Three weeks later, I received an e-mail from a friend of the Professor's letting me know that he had died. Reading the message, I felt bereft, as I had standing on the platform at the train station in Naples, saying good-bye to the Professor after our first few days together on the island of Ischia, ten years ago, when I thought I'd never see him again. But I felt a similar sense of hopefulness, too, as after that delightful chance meeting, a sense of life. The Professor had reminded me whenever I needed reminding that I could still experience *la bella vita,* I could be desired, I could embrace something less than perfection, and, most important, that I could love.

Thank you to William Zinsser, for encouraging me to stop worrying about the publishing world and write what I please. I'm grateful to Kit Miller for giving me time at Orchard House to write, and have fondest memories of Maya Miller, who cheered me on with my daily thousand words. My fellow members of the San Francisco Writers' Grotto, especially Ethan Watters, Tom Barbash, Elizabeth Bernstein, and Po Bronson, gave me invaluable support, suggestions, and community. Many wonderful women offered their wisdom along the way: Cristina Taccone, Cecilia Brunazzi, Cindy Fraser Taylor, Katy Butler, Sharon Salzberg, Martha Borst, Giovanna Tabanelli, Kimberly Easson, and Alyce Musabende. *Saludos* to Anja Fauske, Cheryl Finnegan, and Lamine Thiam in San Miguel de Allende. Zoë Rosenfeld was an amazingly perceptive and helpful reader. Thanks to Suzanne Gluck, Erin Malone, Shaye Areheart, Penny Simon, and everyone at Harmony Books who helped bring this book to light. *Caro Michel, sempre ti ricorderó con molto affetto e spero che ci stia una bella isola per te nel cielo.* Hugs to my parents, Charles and Virginia Fraser, for their constant love and support. And a big kiss to Peter, one of those wonderful Wesleyan men I missed, for looking me up thirty years later.

Laura Fraser is the author of the bestselling memoir *An Italian Affair* and *Losing It,* an investigative look at the weight-loss industry. She is a contributing editor to *More* magazine, and has written for *Gourmet; O, The Oprah Magazine;* the *New York Times; AFAR; Self; Glamour; Vogue; Elle; Redbook; Tricycle Buddhist Review;* and more.